NEW MEXICO CIVIL RIGHTS AND JUSTICE

TEARS IN THE VALLEYS

RAY JOHN DE ARAGÓN

FOREWORD BY RALPH ARELLANES

THE History PRESS

Published by The History Press
An imprint of Arcadia Publishing
Charleston, SC
www.historypress.com

Front cover: *Las Campesinas*, acrylic on canvas, 2019, by Adelita Medina. *Alianza Nacional de Campesinas Collection, Oxnard, California*.

First published 2025

Manufactured in the United States

ISBN 9781467159531

Library of Congress Control Number: 2025931947

Life is but a whisper in the winds of time, but at times, whispers turn into breezes and then powerful winds that strongly affect all of us. The dynamic voice of Sabine Ulibarri, American poet, teacher, writer, critic and statesman, touched everyone. I remember him saying, "Even when my body is cold and lying in a coffin, I will still have something to say." As descendants of the original Spanish families who settled New Mexico in 1598 and who now number in the tens of thousands, we need to continue to tell the stories of our people who came to an unknown land and faced perils on the sea and many hardships, including disease and illness. So many died even though they came with the sole intent and purpose of seeking a new and better life. Sabine Ulibarri—yes, even from his grave—and many others like him continue to tell the stories and dig deep into the roots and history of who we are despite the social injustice endured so that our people will be recognized for their indomitable spirit, perseverance and resilience. These are people our children may look up to and be inspired to follow. Mie Shu Ou, a great American artist born in China and a very close friend, said, "Without having roots, we can never really grow.... Yet I don't think it matters whether our work is in the new or old tradition, it matters only whether it is true or false." The result is "to conceive heaven in a flower, a minimum quality in vastness, and a little fish in a great sea." It is in recognition of these very noteworthy pioneering Spanish settlers of New Mexico, and their many honorable descendants, that this book is respectfully dedicated.

CONTENTS

FOREWORD

When the Spanish first established a permanent settlement in New Mexico near current-day Española in 1598, they wrote the first constitution in this land that eventually became part of the United States of America. One of the first things they wrote in this constitution is that Native American people's lands, water rights and sovereignty would be preserved in perpetuity for their current and future needs. They also wrote that Native American peoples would be treated as equal Spanish citizens with all legal rights as citizens under the Spanish government. After American takeover of the vast New Mexico territory—which also included Arizona, Nevada, parts of Colorado, California, Texas and Utah, with undefined borders—the Spanish constitution was challenged many times in territorial, state and federal courts. Spanish and Mexican land grants and Native lands continue to be challenged up to the present day by the United States court system even though the original constitution was ratified under the Treaty of Guadalupe Hidalgo signed by the governments of Mexico and the United States, which officially ended the Mexican-American War in 1848.

New Mexico's Hispano and Indian communities have fought for land rights via land grants, equality, water rights, educational access, employment rights, environmental justice, civil rights and social justice since that period in New Mexico history. Yet there are few across the country who know about all this continuous struggle because most major media do not cover civil rights issues west of the Mississippi River unless they happen in California.

There have been many past individuals who have carried the torch of civil rights and social justice in New Mexico, such as Reies López Tijerina, Juan José Peña, Donaldo "Tiny" Martínez, George Arellanes, Junio López, José Espiridion Arellanes Jr., J. León Martínez, Fidel "Chief" Gonzales and many others very actively involved through generations of struggle. Our champion educators include Don Félix Martínez, Dr. George I. Sánchez, Dr. Francisco Ángel, Representative Samuel Vigil and so on. Those attempting to take direct energetic action and effect changes in social conditions, poverty and education by speaking out in New Mexico and the rest of the country have come from all walks of life.

The work and powerful efforts of Reies López Tijerina were equal to the work of Cesar Chávez, Dr. Martin Luther King Jr. and Dolores Huerta. Tijerina raised many issues, but mostly, he fought so that our country would acknowledge and honor the Treaty of Guadalupe Hidalgo signed by the United States and Mexico in 1848. Specifically, he fought to uphold our land grants and water rights in New Mexico as outlined and agreed upon by the United States government. Tijerina raised the profile of the land grants issue and made it of national and international importance. He created a national awareness of land, water rights and poverty. He called up these issues and empowered many others across the Southwest to do the same. Reies López Tijerina helped organize the Poor People's March in Washington, D.C., where he marched alongside other national civil rights leaders in the country in the national "Crusade for Justice." This elevated the awareness of poverty in America for minorities and all people in the United States.

In Las Vegas, New Mexico, decorated Vietnam War veteran Juan José Peña organized many marches for Hispanos and veterans' education rights, access and representation of Hispanics in the faculty, staff and administration of New Mexico Highlands University (NMHU). Juan José described the treatment toward Hispanos at NMHU as "strangers in our own land." He often said, "The Chicano Movement has been the sustaining lifeblood of the people of northern New Mexico." He said this after several high-profile Hispanics were bypassed when they applied for the position of president at New Mexico Highlands University. This was a pandemic problem at universities and colleges throughout the United States wherein minorities were shunned when they applied not only for teaching positions but especially administrative posts. Protests erupted at NMHU when student favorite Dr. John Aragón, a finalist, was bypassed for president and a person with minor credentials from Connecticut was instead selected by the board of regents.

On May 31, 1970, the tension at Highlands and communities in the area that provided most of the student population at the university hit a boiling point, and the Hispano/Chicano students at Highlands took over the president's and other administrative offices. The New Mexico State Police and other law enforcement were ready to remove them. Donaldo "Tiny" Martínez was serving as the Fourth Judicial district attorney during this time, and he threatened to have anyone who harmed the students arrested. Roberto Mondragón, the soon-to-be lieutenant governor of the state of New Mexico, also supported the students and opposed police action against them.

The pressure from the students, the community of Las Vegas and most of the population continued to grow and mount over the following year. By January 1, 1971, Bruce King had been elected governor of New Mexico, and he appointed a whole new set of regents. By the fall of 1971, the students, the community of Las Vegas and the people of northern New Mexico had gotten the man they wanted as president of New Mexico Highlands University. Las Vegas native Dr. Francisco Ángel was selected as the first Hispano president of any four-year institution in the United States. Juan José Peña often spoke about this time in his activism. Others who joined in on actively speaking out and participating in this movement included another Vietnam-era veteran, author Ray John de Aragón. Ray John and Juan José both graduated from Robertson High School in Las Vegas in 1964, and both attended NMHU. They, as well as others, felt Hispanics were not adequately represented in colleges and universities.

On June 7, 2023, as the chairman and CEO of the Hispano Roundtable of New Mexico, I spearheaded a petition leading to name a park in Barelas, Albuquerque, the Don Juan José Peña Plaza. The naming was unanimously passed by the mayor and city council, with the vast support of residents. As the current chairman of the Hispano Roundtable of New Mexico, I have held many positions at the local, state and national level, including president of IMAGE de Alburquerque, president of IMAGE de Nuevo Mexico, District 1 director of New Mexico LULAC, state executive director of New Mexico LULAC and the National LULAC co-chairman of the Committee for Social Justice.

LULAC, the National League of Latin American Citizens, was founded in 1929, with affiliates in many states including New Mexico. This group is therefore the oldest and largest Hispanic civil rights organization in the United States. This united group works tirelessly to improve living conditions and opportunities for Hispanics of all origins across the country.

Ralph Arellanes at the Eighty-Eighth Annual LULAC National Convention in San Antonio, Texas, in 2017. Ralph received the National LULAC Social Justice Award. *Photo by Valerie Elicia Arellanes José.*

LULAC was created during a time when most Hispanics were denied basic human rights. This involved the ability to speak up against all injustices that arose from prejudice or racism, including school integration and equal educational opportunities. This struggle involved xenophobia and anti-Hispanic sentiment, which still exist in the nation today. In 1966, LULAC actively supported Cesar Chávez and Dolores Huerta with their United Farm Workers movement, which fought for the civil rights of farmworkers and their families against deplorable working conditions in the nation. This included the rampant and uncontrolled abuse of child labor.

Ralph Arellanes and his wife, Marcella Arellanes, along with their daughter, Valerie Elicia Arellanes José. Valerie was inducted into the National LULAC Woman's Hall of Fame in July 2018 at the national convention in Phoenix, Arizona. *Photo by Ralph Arellanes Jr.*

I have served as the chairman of the Hispano Roundtable of New Mexico for twenty years, which makes me the longest to serve in this capacity. The Hispano Roundtable of New Mexico is a coalition of over fifty partner Hispano organizations with over fifty thousand members of the coalition. The Hispano Roundtable involves organizations at the local, state and national level. It was the foremost community group leading the movement at the New Mexico legislature and other agencies to create and build the National Hispanic Cultural Center in Albuquerque. We also led the movement to construct the building of the World War II Memorial and Monument in Washington, D.C. (1993–2004) and the New Mexico Hispanic Education Act in 2010, the White's Peak land victory in 2010, the Rio Grande del Norte National Monument in 2013 and Organ Mountain Desert Peaks National Monument in 2014. We kept the Bridge and Lottery Scholarship requirements at a 2.5 grade point average (GPA) as opposed to a 3.0 in 2013, created employment agreements with Kirtland

AFB and Sandia National Labs, negotiated the Hispanic Statement of Cooperation (HSOC) in 1995 and 2017 and created a statewide Ethnic Studies Curriculum in 2016. We received White House recognition in 2007, 2008 and 2011 and recognition from President Barack Obama and First Lady Michelle Obama. We helped establish recognition in the U.S. Congressional Record in Washington for Hispano Civil War heroes and battle sites in 2015. The Hispano Roundtable also assisted in establishing a Science, Technology, Engineering, Arts and Mathematics Program with Explora in 2023.

Ray John de Aragón has been a recognized leader and tireless voice for Chicano/Hispanic/Latino civil rights and social justice in New Mexico and around the country for generations. He was a member of the Alianza Federal de las Mercedes (the Federal Alliance of Land Grants), led by charismatic leader Reies López Tijerina. He was actively involved in the struggle to have a Hispanic person named as president of a higher institution at New Mexico Highlands University. Ray John pushed to have Hispanics named to teaching posts and administrative positions at all New Mexico universities and colleges, including the positions of deans of departments. Ray John de Aragón was very actively involved in the trenches during the civil rights movement of the 1960s through the '70s. His book *New Mexico Civil Rights and Justice: Tears in the Valleys* is not only very welcome but also long overdue.

—Ralph Arellanes

Introduction

HISTORICAL SETTING

"*Hoja del árbol no se mueve sin la voluntad de Dios*. (A tree leaf does not move without the grace of God.)" This very beautiful and ancient New Mexico *dicho*, or saying, was emblazoned on a fabulous retablo designed and painted by Marie Romero Cash, a highly recognized master Santera, maker of holy images with a very wide reputation whose pieces and artworks are now recognized the world over. As well as beautiful images, the written word also causes movement.

The decade of the 1960s was marked by social unrest: the Vietnam War, protest marches, racial tension and cultural chaos. Heroic national social justice and civil rights leaders such as Dr. Martin Luther King Jr.; Farm Workers Union President Cesar Chávez, in conjunction with Dolores Huerta; and Reies López Tijerina from New Mexico emerged and led movements decrying the lack of human rights and dignity by demanding equal justice for all. These leaders filled with boundless zeal placed their own lives at risk and inspired the youth. They took up their standards of civil rights. Their voices along with those of their mentors filled the streets and cities across the nation with tens of thousands, and their actions resounded and grew.

When Dr. Martin Luther King Jr.'s very powerful words were spoken on August 28, 1963, in front of the Lincoln Memorial in Washington, D.C., they reverberated around the world: "I have a dream today. I have a dream that one day every valley shall be exalted, every hill and mountain shall be made low, the rough place will be made plain, and the cracked places will be made straight, and the glory of the Lord shall be revealed, and all flesh shall see it together."

Left: United Farmworkers leading woman activist Dolores Huerta has been honored in California and other areas in many ways, including in murals, literature and paintings. In this poster, she is shown with outstretched hands empowering women. *Courtesy Jesús "Chuy" Martínez.*

Below: Each year in Albuquerque, New Mexico, a march is held with banners memorializing civil rights activists Cesar Chávez and Dolores Huerta. Other activities take place at the National Hispanic Cultural Center. *Photo by Arnold Trujillo.*

Cesar Chávez's words were not any less powerful. He echoed King's thoughts, saying, "History will judge societies and governments—and their institutions—not by knowing how big they are or how well they serve the rich and the powerful, but by how effectively they respond to the needs of the poor and the helpless."

Reies López Tijerina's explosive, charismatic force and personal magnetism joined in with the vigorous words of King and Chavez as his voice resonated from the valleys of New Mexico and impacted all Americans across the United States when he passionately stated:

> *The eyes of justice are covered with a blindfold but, yet she sees, and justice will prevail. I have a dream that gives me strength: the happiness of my people. I gladly defend and fight for their rights. My struggle is not in vain. I pray that all the poor will unite, to bring civil rights and justice to New Mexico and all the Southwest. We want justice, not welfare and powdered milk.* Nosotros contamos para algo y reclamando nuestros derechos podemos cambiar todo. *We count for something and by reclaiming our inalienable rights, we can change everything. The silence you hear now, will finally be met with rising shouts for justice!*

In New Mexico, Tijerina was labeled as a firebrand by the news media, which said his voice stirred up the populace into actions they would not otherwise be involved with. However, Tijerina rose up as a giant voice, not only in New Mexico but throughout the Southwest, espousing and standing up for the principles of democracy. This vibrant and highly significant personality took up the torch that was passed on to him. He vibrantly animated the scene at the time with his force and personal magnetism. He delivered his powerful speeches on college campuses, at public gatherings that attracted hundreds and at important organizational functions. Hispanic youth were inspired and got caught up with the fervor and zeal of this remarkable man and period in New Mexico and national history. El Tigre (King Tiger, as Tijerina was called) struggled and shouted out the concerns of a people whose plight had been virtually ignored for countless generations.

An ingrained privilege provided to all authors is the opportunity to list, recognize and express gratitude to those who helped with or inspired a literary work. On June 10, 2000, Ralph Arellanes received the national IMAGE Inc. Civil Rights Leader of the Year Award in a ceremony at the national convention, which was held in San Juan, Puerto Rico. Arellanes was a founding member of the New Mexico Human Rights Coalition. Dr. Irene Blea, a longtime leader in Chicana rights issues, continues to stand up by speaking out on problems affecting all Latina women. Adelita Medina is a former staff member of *El Grito del Norte*, a groundbreaking periodical widely recognized for serving as a platform for Reies López Tijerina, Cesar Chávez and human rights advocates with first-class reporting, stories and photos. Former New Mexico Lieutenant Governor Roberto Mondragón and his company, Aspectos Culturales, and Georgia Roybal took up grassroots stories and published them in *Amigos*, a journal-like series distributed in all grade levels in all New Mexico public schools. Former New Mexico Governors Jerry Apodaca and Tony Anaya spearheaded action as Latino government leaders in the country. Classmate Juan José Peña directed the first Chicano Studies program in the country at New Mexico Highland University. Newspaper writer, reporter and human rights activist José Armas and community organizer Emilia "Milly" Santillanes always spoke up on issues before mayors and city councils and maintained lifelong passions of civil rights they expressed vocally and in writing. Jesús "Chuy" Martínez was a very active member of the United Farmworkers Union under Cesar Chávez in California. He performed songs of the Chicano movement with his guitar in migrant camps and meetings. He is still active with his music and singing, plus hosting popular television programs on history, heritage, culture and traditions. Doria Purcell was an Indian leader of the Red Power Movement in Albuquerque during the 1960s. She always referenced how Native Americans had been used and abused by the English and American governments in history and the present.

On August 27, 1983, I was presented with the Marie Romero Cash retablo/plaque by City of Albuquerque Mayor Harry Kinney and Reyes Newsom, director of the Feria Artesana. This was the largest Hispanic arts festival in the country and was featured in *Newsweek* magazine. I served the event as the literary chairman. Some of the writers I invited and were honored included Rudolfo Anaya, Sabine Ulibarri, Tibo Chávez, Fabiola Cabeza de Baca and Miguel Encinias. Author Jim Sagel wrote a piece on me for the *Feria Artesana Magazine*. Miguel Encinias was the executive director of the Multicultural Enrichment Program at the University of Albuquerque. This university department, with heads from the Native American, Black and Hispanic communities, consisted of trailblazers in bringing forward long-ignored civil rights issues that were not only unheeded but dismissed for countless generations.

This is the story of those terrible days of racial unrest and the people of the past and present who have continued to be those tree leaves inspired by the grace of God to bring about change.

PART I

HOMELAND IN CHAOS

Chapter 1

THE GREY EMINENCE OF TAOS, PRESBÍTERO DON ANTONIO JOSÉ MARTÍNEZ

There are two well-known *dichos*, or sayings, popular in New Mexico. One is "*De tal palo, tal estilla.* (From such a stick, comes splinters.)" Another is "*El hábito no hace al monje.* (The habit does not make the monk.)" Both references apply to what took place in New Mexico and still unfavorably affects the state today. There were adverse consequences that rose up from a sequence of unexpected events. In August 1846, Colonel Stephen Watts Kearny led a large force of Missouri volunteers in an attack on New Mexico Territory. He succeeded in taking the capital city of Santa Fe. The attack was not officially sanctioned by the United States government; it was a preemptive attack ordered by the governor of Missouri. Kearny immediately set up a military dictatorship and organized a system of laws called the Kearny Code, largely patterned after the Missouri Bill of Rights and Laws. Of note was section 2 of his attachments, which read in part, "A creditor wishing to sue his debtor by attachment may place in the clerk's office of the circuit court in the territory…and thereupon such creditors may sue out an original attachment against the lands, tenements, goods, moneys, effects and credits of the debtor in whosoever hands they may be."

This set a precedent for what was to come. The United States entered a war with Mexico that ended with the signing of the Treaty of Guadalupe Hidalgo in 1848. The territory of New Mexico—which had ambiguous boundaries that covered Arizona, Nevada, parts of Colorado and Texas and even went into California—was incorporated into the United States as an organized territory in an Organic Act on September 9, 1850. Tenuous interpretations of the Kearny Code, the treaty provisions and the Organic Act struck a severe blow to the civil rights and entitlements of New Mexico Hispanic and Native American citizens.

Before and during the Mexican-American War, hatred and animosity toward Mexico proliferated in the United States. This was spurred on by newspapers, politicians and word of mouth. Racist statements were aimed against Mexico and anything Mexican, primarily the people. The ones hardest hit by this animosity were the government officials, military commanders and religious leaders. Political cartoons, caricatures, songs, illustrations, books and articles showed the Mexican masses as ignorant, primitive and useless ne'er-do-wells. For example, Congressman Truman Smith of Connecticut announced on the House floor of Congress that New Mexico was

> *under the control of the clergy to an extraordinary degree. The standard of morals is exceedingly low….The country is little better than a Sodom….I am free to say that if all the vices which can corrupt the human heart, and all the qualities which reduce man to the life of a brute, are to be "annexed" to the virtue and intelligence of the American people, I DO NOT DESIRE TO BELONG TO ANY SUCH UNION.*

One clergyman Congressman Smith most probably was referring to was Padre Antonio José Martínez of New Mexico. This priest served as a representative of New Mexico Territory in the Mexican National Congress. On November 28, 1843, Padre Martínez wrote a treatise to the president of Mexico with the title "An Exposition of Things in New Mexico." It was published and distributed throughout the nation. The priest stated that French American traders and others were selling and trading massive amounts of whiskey to the Indians. This was resulting in the Indian nations trading buffalo hides for alcohol. Indians in New Mexico, to satisfy their appetite for intoxicating beverages, began to deal more and more with the traders. They were then stealing cattle, attacking settlements, raiding and pillaging defenseless settlements. The proprietors of American forts that were situated near the borders of New Mexico Territory stimulated these depredations with barrels of whiskey. The popular priest believed the Americans were turning intelligent and industrious Indians, who were citizens of Mexico, into individuals with no desire to occupy their time with various arts or industries, to raise cattle or to cultivate their vast lands. The priest's exposition apparently came to the attention of the United States government, since copies were also distributed to officials in New Mexico. Congressman Truman Smith loudly stated:

> *The priest proclaims he is a country-loving citizen with the high privilege which directs free speech, and he would like these people to be governed by ideas equal to all citizens of this country....In short, they are morally, physically, and intellectually distanced in the great race of improvement which is run in almost every quarter of the earth. Give them but* tortillas, frijoles, *and* chile colorado *to supply their animal wants for the day, and seven tenths of the Mexicans are satisfied....If we are to take over this land, we must first replace the priests who have too much control over their people.*

Catholicism had existed in New Mexico for nearly two centuries. Some Indian tribes had been Christianized by Spanish Franciscan frays. The concerns of Padre Martínez were well known, especially when they involved the poor in general and the Native Americans in particular. After Mexico gained its independence from Spain, over one hundred secular priests ministered in New Mexico. Most were ordained in Durango, Mexico. The Church in New Mexico was under the Diocese of Durango and was guided by Bishop José Antonio Laureano de Zubiria y Escalante. His vicar in New Mexico was Monsignor Juan Felipe Ortiz. Tithing since Spanish colonial times was in the form of fruits of the earth to support the Church, including meat, vegetables, fruit and handiwork. The settlers built the churches and chapels and helped maintain them through generations. This was seen in families as an integral part of their Catholic faith, even on Pueblo Indian settlements. The new Republic of Mexico introduced a monetary system of tithing. Padre Antonio José Martínez, a leading priest in New Mexico, bitterly opposed the mandatory tithing because it was a particular burden on the poor. Due to his efforts, mandatory money tithings were removed by the Mexican congress. He was hailed as a hero in New Mexico Territory and Mexico.

In 1850, Pope Pius IX elevated a young French American priest by the name of Jean Baptiste Lamy, who was assigned to the parish of Covington, Kentucky, to the position of bishop of New Mexico. Church life in France flourished during this pope's pontificate. Jean Baptiste Lamy served for short periods in a few parishes in the United States before the surprise announcement. Lamy took along a boyhood friend, Joseph Projectus Machebeuf, who had been ordained into the priesthood at the same time as his new vicar general, to New Mexico. Since many French fur trappers and traders had infiltrated New Mexico for many years, Lamy and Machebeuf found ready and enthusiastic supporters among them. This would prove helpful since neither Lamy nor Machebeuf knew how to speak Spanish, the language of the vast territory.

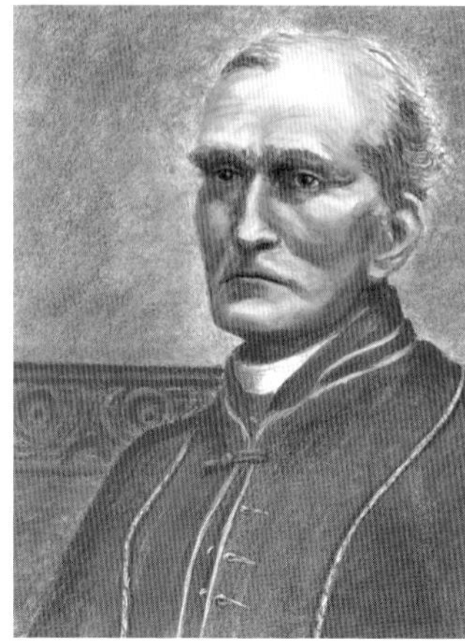

In fiction, Franco-American Bishop Jean Baptiste Lamy was described as a pioneering Catholic prelate sent to discipline the immorality and rampant unrestraint of Hispanics in New Mexico Territory. In stark contrast, Lamy was self-righteous and domineering and completely disregarded the rights of the Roman Catholic residents and the Indians he saw as wild and uncivilized. *Author's collection.*

Jean Baptiste Lamy and Joseph Projectus Machebeuf both had biased and prejudiced mindsets about New Mexico and the native priests. They firmly believed they were going into a wild frontier to clean up a "Sodom of immorality." In brief, Bishop Lamy replaced the Native clergy with French priests. In fact, Frenchmen dominated the clergy in New Mexico after he succeeded in attracting newly ordained priests from France. Bishop Lamy felt he needed obedient priests, especially after he passed an edict in 1854 requiring mandatory monetary tithing from all Catholics in New Mexico. His edict and pronouncements read in the churches stipulated fees for all sacraments, including baptisms, confirmations, weddings and funeral rites. The French bishop wrote:

> *The faithful must obey all instructions and all obligations. My wish is not to be forced to impose severe penalties for the disobedience of those who failed to comply. Those that continue in their disobedience will not receive the sacraments and they will be considered as being outside of the fold. Your immoral ways will lead to divine punishment.* Fandangos *are conducive to evil, occasions of sin, they provide opportunities for immoral relationships that are reprehensible and sinful….Your dances represent a school of immorality and vice. All New Mexicans who attend the profane diversion have lost their fear of God, their innocence and honor. Be not deceived, neither fornicators, nor adulterers, nor highwaymen, nor those given to drinking, nor blasphemers, nor thieves, shall inherit the kingdom of God.*

There was an immediate cultural clash between the French American bishop and the vast Roman Catholic population of New Mexico that had developed since the territory was settled by Spain in 1598. Bishop Lamy disliked the adobe Spanish Pueblo architecture of the territory. He thought of replacing the ancient churches with French-style buildings. By tithing the people, he felt he could secure the necessary funds to erect new churches. The San Francisco Church in Santa Fe, built in 1714, was his first target for building a massive cathedral worthy of his position as the prelate of the new diocese. Spanish traditions, heritage, culture and history were totally ignored by Lamy. If his coffers were filled, then he would be satisfied. According to him, the end justified the means. Immediate and extended family members had to pay the tithing for anyone who failed to pay the tithes for church services. Triple amounts would build up if the tithes went unpaid. Lamy hired a crew of collectors who traveled throughout the territory, kept accounts and reported back to him. Vicar General Machebeuf also traveled to the towns and churches and reported back to the bishop in Santa Fe.

The loss of lands by the Hispanic and Indian residents of New Mexico after the Mexican-American War was devastating. Impoverished areas where people were deprived of natural resources, their homes, farms, ranches, schools, religious houses of worship and even cemeteries were created by the government and the new American prelate of New Mexico, Bishop Jean Baptiste Lamy. The people were exposed to a quagmire of legalistic terms dealing with property and landownership under the laws of the United States government. Technical terms that were often difficult to comprehend or understand made it easy to grab lands that had been held for centuries by both Hispanic and Indian residents of New Mexico. Under Spain and later the Mexican Republic, the process of landownership was much clearer.

Tensions rose up to the point of a revolt against Bishop Lamy and his harsh treatment of the people. He operated with an iron fist. Each time a Native priest would object—especially when he cut down church services to once a month, including the Catholic Mass—the bishop would censure the priest and defrock him. In many cases, Bishop Lamy used excommunication to force New Mexico Catholics to comply with his wants and desires. Complaints flowed to the Vatican in Rome. However, Bishop John Baptist Purcell, who was later elevated to cardinal in Cincinnati, Ohio, whom Lamy confided in, ran interference and intervened constantly on his behalf at the Vatican. The American Church strongly supported Lamy and his heavy-handed actions.

In conjunction with tithing, Lamy seized what he considered church properties, including the homes of defrocked priests and their families and private chapels constructed by the people. He succeeded in taking over La Castrense, the Spanish military chapel that was claimed by the new American government in Santa Fe. He had the chapel torn down and sold the property. Any buildings and lands he acquired, whether legally or illegally, were sold for building materials shipped over from France and to pay French workers and others from Missouri to build his cathedral.

Through all this, the thorn in Bishop Lamy's back was Padre Antonio José Martínez of Taos. Lamy closed the school, orphanage and seminary the priest had established in 1833 in Taos under Bishop Zubiria. Several Native New Mexico priests had received training in his Our Lady of Guadalupe Seminary and were ordained by Zubiria. Political and religious dynamics played into the hands of Bishop Jean Baptiste Lamy. Under Napoleon III, France invaded Mexico in 1861 but did not capture the capital city of Mexico until 1862. The United States government avoided direct conflict with France and sought an agreeing relationship. Lamy obviously felt more confident and secure in his actions and sought French government support. He then freely used his purported powers of excommunication as a threat of excluding anyone or everyone who did not comply with his decrees or commands. As to payment of tithes for religious services, he was unwavering in his mandates. Not to tithe meant exclusion from all sacraments of the Church, including baptism, reconciliation, eucharist, confirmation, matrimony, anointing of the sick and extreme unction. These people would then be eternally banished from the Catholic Church. The mentality of the period was eternal damnation.

Lamy did excommunicate many of the faithful, and even entire villages, but promised to restore them to the Church if they should plead for mercy and recant. Those who strenuously objected and attempted to bring the bishop's despotic actions to the attention of the pope in Rome fell on deaf ears. These actions made Lamy more determined. Indian tribes were prohibited from holding ceremonial dances. Church services in rural areas, including Indian *pueblos*, were reduced to once a month. When Bishop Lamy learned that Padre Antonio José Martínez of Taos was still ministering as usual in the missions and was providing funds for the payment of tithes out of necessity for the poor, he considered Martínez and his followers recalcitrant priests in need of serious discipline. Padre Martínez was a highly regarded expert in both canon law and civil law. His abilities in jurisprudence were highly recognized even by the American government.

West Las Vegas Schools elementary students drew a picture story of the life and times of New Mexico folk hero priest Padre Antonio José Martínez. This child showed a baby carriage in New Mexico to express his birth in 1793. *Author's collection.*

In fact, Martínez had served as the president of the First Constitutional Convention held in Santa Fe in 1849. When Bishop Lamy approached the government in Santa Fe to pass a law making it a crime to withhold payment of tithes to the Church and the idea was rejected, he said, "The legislative assembly is composed of ignorant men, most of them corrupt, dishonest, who hold the people in fear of them…and the corruption of this society illustrates their prejudice toward a foreign bishop who is obliged to reform their morals."

Don Antonio José Martínez, New Mexico's folk hero priest, was often referred to as *presbítero*, which translates to "presbyter," meaning a priest or minister in English. However, some writers took it as meaning an elder of the Presbyterian Church and wrote that the priest was in a schism with the Catholic Church. *Courtesy Dora Martínez y Armijo.*

Padre Antonio José Martínez incurred the wrath of the bishop in various ways. Lamy undermined the abilities of the priest and was determined to remove him. However, the old priest of Taos paid his respects to the bishop and attempted to state his case as he had done before with the Mexican government. Meetings and letters failed to deter the bishop from his actions. Therefore, Padre Martínez apparently felt his only recourse was to write his pleadings, which were published in the leading newspaper, *La Gazeta de Santa Fe* (the *Santa Fe Gazette*). This had worked in Mexican newspapers. Padre Martínez had introduced the first printing press west of the Mississippi and published the first newspaper, *El Crepúsculo de la Libertad* (the *Dawn of Liberty*). He felt a literate society was an advanced society. Some of his students became Spanish newspaper publishers, attorneys and judges. Bishop Lamy was in a quandary as to how to deal with this stubbornly resistant priest who objected to his selling lands, buildings and homes that had been donated to the Catholic Church. Padre Martínez also objected to the prohibition of Indian ceremonials and regular fiestas and celebrations that had been held since Spanish colonial days in all New Mexico communities. Bishop Lamy made very few pastoral visits in New Mexico Territory but did make several trips back to France. He would leave Machebeuf in charge to dispense his proclamations and remove the Native priests and enforce his mandates. Padre Martínez constantly reminded the bishop he was not following canon law or any proper judicial proceedings, pastoral promulgations or church rules. Bishop Lamy finally felt compelled to send his vicar general to Our Lady of Guadalupe Church in Taos, where Padre Martínez served as pastor, and proclaim the padre as excommunicated and defrocked. Padre Martínez continued to minister to the faithful until his death in 1869.

The "Holy Grail" that defines the work of master artist Huberto Maestas is a larger-than-life bronze sculpture of folk hero priest Padre Antonio José Martínez located in Taos. It is a leading attraction in the area. *Photo by Santiago Pacheco.*

Father Alberto Gallegos of the Basilica of Our Lady of Sorrows in Chicago, a leading and recognized historian and scholar on Roman Catholic Church history and canon law, wrote in his published work in 1978, *Canon Law and Excommunication*, "The excommunication of Padre Antonio José Martínez was not conducted according to canon law and because of that fact alone, his excommunication was, and always has been illegal and invalid."

Eminent New Mexico state historian Dr. Myra Ellen Jenkins once wrote about the famous folk hero priest of Taos, Padre Don Antonio José Martínez, memorialized by a bronze statue and many accolades after his death:

> *In every culture, particularly during periods of social ferment and political and economic stress, powerful personalities have emerged who—by virtue of their convictions, forcefully expressed by word and pen, and often translated into action—have influenced and helped direct the course of history and events.*
>
> *One such leader in New Mexico throughout the turbulent mid-1800s was Antonio José Martínez, priest of Taos. For nearly half a century this dynamic, outspoken, and controversial cleric was undoubtedly New Mexico's most influential native son. This era of his influence covered*

the entire period of sovereignty exercised by a new Mexican national government over its northern frontier; a national government struggling to find itself, only to be cut short by United States occupation and military control, followed by Territorial status.

Shortly after his ordination, Padre Martínez was assigned to his own parish in Taos, where his wealthy father was one of the largest landowners. Martínez quickly gained the trust of his spiritual charges by his tireless rounds of distant churches scattered throughout the extensive Taos valley including several Indian pueblos such as the venerable Taos pueblo Church of San Gerónimo.

As a Mexican patriot Padre Martínez realized that republican principles could never be attained by an illiterate and uninformed citizenry. Hence, he established a school and acquired the only press in the territory, on which he printed his printing materials. He also used the press to make known his positions on public issues to authorities in Santa Fe and even to the president of Mexico. Nor did he hesitate to use his ecclesiastical position, his political influence and the power of his pen and press to do battle with the extranjeros, *those Anglo and French-Canadian traders who attempted to secure a virtual monopoly over the economic life of the region.*

Despite the forced change of national allegiance from Mexico to the United States in 1846–48, the priest continued to be elected by his faithful constituents to legislative bodies and to champion matters of social concern. His espousal of traditional church practices in opposition to the mandates of French-born Bishop Jean Baptiste Lamy ended in excommunication. Antonio José Martínez has rightfully earned his position as New Mexico's folk hero.

Paul Horgan, in his book *Lamy of Santa Fe*, quoted the bishop as saying about his tenure of ministry in New Mexico Territory:

Our Mexican population has quite a sad future. Very few of them will be able to follow modern progress. They cannot be compared to the Americans in the way of intellectual liveliness, ordinary skills, and industry; they will thus be scorned and considered an inferior race. If the bishop who will follow me has not lived among the Mexicans for a long time and if he should not show a strong interest in them, they will become disheartened. Seeing themselves on the one hand under American discipline and on the other, imagining that the Americans prefer foreigners to them, their faith, which is still lively enough, would grow gradually weaker; and the consequences

> *would be dreadful. The morals, manners, and customs of our unfortunate people are quite different from those of the Americans. With the best possible intentions, those who would not try to understand our worshipers or would become interested in their well-being, would have trouble adapting to their spirit, which is almost too primitive.*

When Willa Cather released what some have touted as the great American novel, *Death Comes for the Archbishop*, in 1927, others in New Mexico saw it as a racist book. The reason is because Cather chose to distort New Mexico and malign the people. First, she used made-up names for the protagonists and falsified historical actions; second, she used the actual names of people as the antagonists and placed communities and events in real historical context and changed things in a faithless manner. University English students were required to read Cather's book and write reports. Of course, English professors saw the book as a classic of American literature and of lasting historical and artistic worth.

Some of what Willa Cather wrote in her very popular and famous work included:

> *It* [New Mexico] *still pitifully calls itself a Catholic country and tries to keep the forms of religion without instruction.... The few priests are without guidance or discipline, and some of them live in open concubinage. If this Augean stable is not cleansed, now that the territory has been taken over by a progressive government, it will prejudice the interests of the church in the whole of North America.*

Cather went on to describe Padre Martínez through the eyes of the hero, Bishop Latour, by saying:

> *His broad shoulders were like a bull buffalo's, his big head was set defiantly on a thick neck, and the full-cheeked, richly colored, egg-shaped Spanish face—how vividly the bishop remembered that face! It was so unusual that he would be glad to see it again; a high, narrow forehead, brilliant yellow eyes set deep in strong arches, and full, florid cheeks,—not blank areas of smooth flesh, as in Anglo-Saxon faces, but full of muscular activity, as quick to change with feeling as any of his features. His mouth was the very assertion of violent, uncurbed passions and tyrannical self-will; the lips thrust out and taut, like the flesh of animals distended by fear and desire.*

Cather then set the stage for what would shock her readers. It can be said readers in the late 1920s would have been appalled reading anything that went against the precepts of the Church coming from any cleric that would have been considered sacred at the time. She meant it to be a contrast between a very holy French bishop as compared to a very unholy Mexican priest who not only had no morals but also taught his congregation against anything that had to do with what were regarded as proper Christian principles.

Cather goes on to say that Padre Martínez did not know how to read and write until he was an adolescent. She claims he hated all Americans because they would put an end to his being the lord of all his subjects and that the priest had corrupted a fifteen-year-old girl. According to her, when he was younger, Padre Martínez played the part of a Don Juan; in other words, the padre was freewheeling and completely lacking in self-restraint as he chased girls. Under the bishop's jurisdiction, which Padre Martínez did not abide by, he became a schismatic, one drawn away from the Roman Catholic Church by starting his own religion. Therefore, the bishop had no other recourse than to remove that "cancerous tumor" when Padre Martínez and another Mexican cleric organized their own church. Padre Martínez's schismatic church was too much for Bishop Vaillant to bear. He stripped Padre Martínez of all the rights and privileges of the priesthood through excommunication.

Historical fiction is a narrative that takes place in the past and characterizes by an imaginative reconstruction of historical people and events. Willa Cather is considered one of the best and most important writers of the twentieth century. Her *Death Comes for the Archbishop* was a bestseller and is thought of by critics as a masterpiece of American literature. Reviewers have also praised Cather's book highly. In fact, her book of fiction has been referred to as important to historians and scholars studying the life and times of New Mexico history.

A New Mexico Folk Hero and Legend

Padre Antonio José Martínez was respected and honored by the Indians, immigrants of all races who arrived in New Mexico and his own people. The Natives thought of the priest as a Great Holy Man with infinite powers who always sought to protect them. Padre Martínez was the supporter and protector of the poor and disadvantaged. His smile, words and open arms rekindled the hopes and aspirations of all southwestern people, and that is why in the moment they lost him forever, on July 27, 1867, everyone cried without consolation. They prayed for him and dedicated final memories that were written in grains of sand and soil.

A memorial was held for this beloved priest of the people on July 28, 1867, attended by a large multitude in Taos. A French American proclaimed sadly, "He is gone; the priest that served everyone that needed him, with his ministry, with his money, and with heartwarming counsel, is gone. No one ever left his side without leaving spiritually richer."

Anthony Joseph, originally from St. Louis, Missouri, who counted the Taos priest as one of his tutors, stated, "He was an exemplary person, worthy of imitation by everyone."

The entire body of the New Mexico Territorial Legislature called the deceased priest "the Honor of his country." People from throughout New Mexico Territory traveled countless miles to attend the funeral of Padre Antonio José Martínez. It is written that various groups belonging to penitential orders, popularly known as the Penitentes, officiated at the priest's wake and continuously sang doleful hymns called *alabados* before and during the funeral. Taos and the territory had never seen such a gathering of people, numbering in the hundreds and of mixed races.

Highly acclaimed artist, playwright, theatrical producer and director Rosa María Calles has captivated audiences with her work. Calles has introduced a new visual awareness to the history and traditions as well as the struggles of Hispanics in New Mexico. The theatrical performance of the *Grey Eminence of Taos* sought to portray the factual events surrounding the life of the famous priest on stage. *Courtesy Rosa María Calles.*

"El Corrido de Padre Don Antonio José Martínez"
By Rosa María Calles

Esta es una historia de un hombre fino y valiente.
Todos lo llamaban Conciliador de la gente.
Era El Conciliador de todos los pobres y ancianos,
A todas las razas, niños, y paisanos.

Antonio José era hijo de Severino Martínez y María del Carmen,
Nació en el día de San Antonio
en el Pueblo de Abiquiú en Nuevo México.
Todos estaban llenos de alegría y cantaban cu cu ru cu cu.

Su maestro fue Gerónimo Becerra.
Era estudiante muy brillante y cualquiera
Conocía su Espíritu y su capacidad,
Y pasar los años, creció con integridad.

La prenda de su amor fue María de la Luz
Tuvieron sus bodas, pero también una cruz.
María murió al nacer una hija,
Antonio le dijo, yo te cuido mi hijita.

El hijo obediente trabajo mucho en el rancho
Asistiendo el ganado, y la siembra con cuidado.
Entre tanto Antonio José decidió dedicarse
A su Dios y la mama, la Virgen María.

Se fue a Durango en México,
Aprendió mucho de la ley y Justicia
Entre tanto fue ordenado sacerdote.
Estaba lleno de dedicación y alegría.

Pero el nuevo padrecito sufrió otra vez.
Perdió su hija y luego su papa,
y se dedicó a su ministerio,
dando su vida con toda su fuerza.

Bendita la genta que él sirvió
con derechos civiles, y a la justicia sin faltar,
Con su parroquia y con sus misiones,
y a todos por igual.

Llego el día de su testamento,
Dios se llevó al Conciliador al Cielo,
La voz de la gente ceso de vivir
La voz de todo paro de existir.

El Campeón era el héroe de los pobres,
El defensor de los indios,
El padrecito de toda la gente,
Que vive siempre en nuestro corazón
El brillante Padre Antonio José con toda razón.

"The Ballad of Padre Don Antonio José Martínez"
By Rosa María Calles

This is the story of a fine and valiant man.
Everyone called him Conciliator of the people.
He was the Conciliator of all the poor and the elderly
To all races, children, and countrymen.

Antonio José was the son of Severino Martínez and María del Carmen
He was born on the feast day of St. Anthony
In the town of Abiquiu in New Mexico.
Everyone was full of joy and sang cu cu ru cu cu.

His teacher was Geronimo Becerra,
He was a brilliant student and everyone
recognized his spirit and ability.
As years passed, he grew with integrity.

The jewel of his love was Maria de la Luz
They had their wedding, but it ended in pain.
Maria died in childbirth when their daughter was born,
Antonio said I'll take care of you my little daughter.

The dutiful son worked hard at the ranch
Caring for the livestock, and the gardens with attention.
In time Antonio Jose decided to dedicate himself
To God and mother, the Blessed Virgin Mary.

He went to Durango in Mexico,
He learned a lot about law and civil justice
And was ordained a priest.
He was full of dedication and joy.

But the poor priest suffered once again.
Antonio Jose lost his daughter and then his father,
And dedicated himself to his ministry
Giving his life with all his vigor.

Blessed were the people that he served,
With civil rights, and to justice without failing
In his parish and his missions
And everyone equally.

The day came for his last testament,
God took the Conciliator to Heaven,
The voice of the people ceased to live
The voice of everything ceased to exist.

The champion was the hero of the poor,
The defender of the Indians,
The priest of the people,
May he live always in our hearts,
The brilliant Don Antonio José Martínez.

Chapter 2

LAS GORRAS BLANCAS

GRASSROOTS STRUGGLES

Anytime, anywhere groups appear that seem militant in nature with proponents seemingly aiming toward violence to attain their goals, such as Malcolm X and the Black Panthers, they are disdained, especially by the news media. Such was the case with a very active group known as Las Gorras Blancas, loosely translated as the White Caps, numbering in the thousands in northern New Mexico in the late nineteenth century and into the early twentieth century.

I first heard of Las Gorras Blancas from my mother, María Cleofas Sánchez de Aragón, who was originally from a village known as Peñasco Blanco near Mora, New Mexico. My mother always referred to this group as heroes of our people and spoke very highly of them. My mother claimed these men composed of Hispanic ranchers and farmers from northern New Mexico sought justice for what she called lands that were stolen from our people. No entity had the authority to usurp vested interests in landownership. This included Indian lands and lands granted by the Spanish government or Mexican government by recognized grants to individuals or communities. Any person or persons seeking a grant of land petitioned the local alcalde, or mayor, who then submitted the written petition to the governor. A statement regarding the availability of pastureland, water and trees for lumber and firewood would be addressed. It also had to be available land not claimed by others, nor could the grant infringe on Indian lands. Early Spanish and later Mexican maps showed extensive areas of lands controlled by the tribes. All Spanish colonial towns and villages in New Mexico developed through community land grants provided to several families who petitioned together to the Spanish and later Mexican governments. Boundaries were described as natural borders such as hills, a nearby Indian settlement, a mesa, a ridge, a river, a bosque or another grant given to another individual or community.

Our family home was located on Hot Springs Boulevard on a main road leading to the Old Town Plaza Park about three and a half blocks south. Back in those early days, the wide dirt road was called North Pacific Street. My mother said family recollections were that up to one hundred or more riders on horseback would pass by the house on the way to the park at night. There, the riders would gather with other men carrying torches and spend time deciding on and working out a plan. They all had their heads covered with short white cloths with two holes cut open for their eyes. The cloths were meant to conceal their identities. After determining a plan, they would ride off in different directions to execute their method of achieving their goal.

In 1878, the Atchison Topeka and Santa Fe (AT&SF) Railroad system, with extensive lines in the vast territory of New Mexico, officially opened with joyous celebrations in Santa Fe and other cities. However, this celebration was at the expense of populations of Hispanics and Indians in many areas that adversely affected their lives. In many communities across the territory, this was a history filled with hardships, struggles and deep sorrow. The final establishment of this railway system through northern New Mexico, which included parts of southern Colorado, was an unsettled period of violence, despair and even death. Entire communities were uprooted. Indian villages were removed. Hispanic farmers and ranchers lost their livelihoods. Dense forests were destroyed, and wild game disappeared. Crops were burned, and rivers and other water sources were at times purposely polluted; therefore, lives were ruined and poverty became rampant across New Mexico.

Many men became extremely wealthy due to wheeling and dealing. Hired gunslingers were prevalent. A group known collectively as the Santa Fe Ring viciously ruled the territory. The Ring powerhouse was in the capital city of Santa Fe. This notorious and blatantly corrupt group of unscrupulous individuals was composed of governors, greedy government officials, judges, politicians and lawmen. Many of them were southern sympathizers or Confederate officers and soldiers. Included were remnants of Confederate troops who suffered a humiliating defeat at the famous Battle of Glorieta at the hands of the New Mexico Volunteers in 1862. New Mexico forces were composed mostly of Hispanic soldiers who answered the call of duty by providing their own horses, munitions and arms and food supplies in the cause of defending the Union. The Confederacy lost the battle in New Mexico. This eventually led to the Confederate States losing the War of the Rebellion.

Some of the written history of New Mexico is selective. A few historians have selected only parts of what they choose to write about. This includes how the building of the AT&SF Railroad affected the people. Vast amounts of timber were obviously necessary. Lumber was required for railroad ties, which were laid crosswise to secure railway tracks. Thousands of trees were cut down to provide the ties. Other lumber was needed to provide temporary housing for the workers and facilities for cooks, saloons and saloon girls. Forests were located on lands belonging to New Mexico communities and the residents. Hundreds of workers needed to be fed, so buffalo herds and deer plus cattle and sheep provided meat. Chickens provided eggs, and milk cows were also required, along with other foodstuffs such as fruit and vegetables. Rivers and other sources of water were also located on private properties. Railroad officials were faced with a quandary. Hispanic residents had no intention of selling rights-of-way for the railroad.

Maneuvers came in the form of uncontrolled land theft. Anglo territorial leaders had inside information as to the areas the railway system was to run through. Surveying and mapping had already taken place. Conniving individuals met secretly in Santa Fe to determine a plan and course of action. Newspaper reports called Las Gorras Blancas clandestine vigilantes who preyed on innocent victims and were involved in terrorizing the countryside, pillaging and vandalizing. To counter these claims, anonymous letters were sent out and fliers were distributed by the group detailing their struggles and complaints. The print media of the day stimulated animosity, and telegraph messages increased in the territory warning state officials about the dark clouds heading their way. Las Gorras Blancas leaders issued an official declaration to counter misinformation.

The following proclamation was published in the *Las Vegas Daily Optic* on March 12, 1890, around the year Las Gorras Blancas was organized:

> *Our purpose is to protect the rights and interest of the people in general; especially those of the helpless classes. We want the Las Vegas Grant settled to the benefit of all concerned, and this we hold is the entire community within the grant. We want no "land grabs" or obstructionists of any sort to interfere. We will watch them. We are not down on lawyers as a class, but the usual knavery and unfair treatment of the people must be stopped. Our judiciary hereafter must understand that we will sustain it*

Juan José, Pablo and Nicanor Herrera, shown here in 1889, are credited with organizing Las Gorras Blancas, a large group of ranchers and farmers in northern New Mexico who sought justice for stolen land grants. *Courtesy Diane Stein, Los Artesanos.*

> *only when "justice" is the password. The practice of "double dealing" must cease. There is a wide difference between New Mexico's "law" and "justice." And justice is God's law, and that we must have at all hazards. We are down on racial issues, will watch race agitation. We are all human*

> *brethren, under the same glorious flag. We favor irrigation enterprises but will fight any scheme that tends to monopolize the supply of water courses to the detriment of residents living on lands watered by the same streams. We favor all enterprises, but object to corrupt methods to further same. We don't care how much you get so long as you do it fairly and honestly. The people are suffering from the effects of partisan "bossism" and those bosses had better quietly hold their peace. The people have been persecuted and hacked about in every which way to satisfy their caprice. If they persist in their usual methods retribution will be their reward. We are watching "political informers." We have no grudge against any person, but we are the enemies of bulldozers and tyrants. We must have a free ballot and a fair count. And the will of the majority shall be respected. Intimidations and the "indictment" plan have no further fear for us. If the old system should continue, death would be a relief to our sufferings. And for our rights our lives are the least we can pledge. If the fact that we are law abiding citizens is questioned, come to our homes and see the hunger and desolation we are suffering; and "this" is the result of deceitful and corrupt methods of "bossism."*

There was a time when everyone had access to communal lands. Millions of acres and all their resources were available to all people. This was in the form of rivers, streams, game and fishing. Under the Spanish and Mexican governments, these lands were not only held in common but also helped sustain the welfare and well-being of the Native Americans and Hispanic Natives of New Mexico. With the American takeover, all of this changed. Access to the lands was shut off by establishing land reserves. This provided the opportunity for the creation of land barons. A repressive territorial authority came into being across New Mexico. Intimidation and incursion were rampant. In response to massive injustices across the land, a group of farmers and ranchers developed an organized movement in 1889 to fight against land speculators and opportunists who invaded New Mexico. Recognized leaders of this resistance group, called Las Gorras Blancas, were three brothers named Juan José, Pablo and Nicanor Herrera. They were heirs along with many others to the community Las Vegas Land Grant, which had gone down from a total of 500,000 acres to a few thousand. The land was recognized as prime territory that held lush forests, substantial water, green fields, other vegetation and wild game, including bison, deer and fowl. As more land was expropriated and land barons took over, poverty and hunger in the area increased without control. Barbed wire was strung

Las Gorras Blancas, a historic narrative of social justice painting by Rock Ulibarri. The artist captured details surrounding the town of Las Vegas, New Mexico, and the land theft that took place in the Las Vegas Land Grant. *Courtesy of Rock Ulibarri.*

up everywhere. This created the saying among the people, "*Con el alambre vino el hambre*. (With barbed wire came hunger.)" Juan José Herrera also created an organization called Los Caballeros de Labor, the Knights of Labor. This was the first farmworkers' union in the country. The group objected to the fact that fields numbering in the hundreds of acres, many planted with vegetables and fruit trees, were suddenly lost. Sheep flocks were slaughtered and replaced with massive herds of cattle and scores of cowboy/gunslingers riding the ranges.

From 1885 until the turn of the century, the secret organization of masked night riders called Las Gorras Blancas struck with dauntless tenacity. They cut the fences and burned railroad ties to stop the railroad from going through their fields. This movement had great public support. It is interesting to note that capitalist adventurers created a corporation called the Las Vegas Land and Cattle Company to pursue their goals of taking over the original grant lands. The same successful trick was used in other areas of New Mexico. There was the Nicolas Duran y Chávez Land Grant Company, which used proxies and powers of attorney to access thousands of acres and make millions of dollars in the process. The same took place with the Tome Land Grant Company, which made the news for theft of lands from the original heirs. It was not altogether surprising that many people protected the members of Las Gorras Blancas until someone turned the Herrera brothers in. Juan José Herrera was captured and sentenced to prison. Las Vegas Judge Thomas Smith issued a "Dead or Alive" warrant for Pablo Herrera; he was killed. Without strong leadership and with other members fearing for their lives and welfare of their families, the social justice activities of a group of possibly five thousand riders began to disintegrate. Their wives and children were targeted. But this historic episode in Las Vegas, San Miguel County, New Mexico, also violently touched other areas in the territory.

There was a peaceful village named La Placita del Rio Bonito (the little town of the pretty river). This town, which was located next to a winding river with clear sparkling waters, was a joy to behold for anyone traveling by there. Nearby ranches and farms were located on land granted to the settlers by the Spanish and later Mexican governments. Livestock included cattle and horses that grazed on the lush green fields. In the town square, a *torreón* stood out, tall and imposing. This was a round stone defensive tower covered with a mud finish. A large wall surrounded this enclave. All early New Mexico Spanish colonial villages possessed these towers, which served to protect everyone when the area was being attacked by marauding Indians, who were primarily the Apache, Comanche and Navajo. The church was in town, plus a couple of small family-run mercantile establishments that provided other necessities beyond vegetables and fruit. Everyone there was pretty much family or thought of each other that way. But then things began to change. Outsiders thought of this as a golden land of opportunity. Others moved in, such as an Englishman named John Tunstall. Before him, it was James Dolan and Lawrence Murphy, who were Irishmen. All three set up massive mercantile businesses selling guns, ammo and other items often found only in large cities. Many additional strangers like John Chisum and Tom Catron, leader of the Santa Fe Ring, also got involved. Chisum became the largest cattleman in New Mexico Territory and then the entire Southwest. Original residents lost landholdings. The town's name was changed to Lincoln, and the area that was part of extensive San Miguel County became Lincoln County.

The Horrell brothers—Tom, Merritt, Matt, Ben and Sam—freshly out of Texas along with a couple dozen or more men, entered the picture. Some of them had served in the Confederate army. The brothers and their men set up Horrell Ranch upstream of the Pecos River. Saloons were part of the new businesses in Lincoln. After doing some drinking, they killed two prominent Hispanic ranchers. Most of the story has been left out of the pages of history, ether deliberately or by chance. It is known that on December 1, 1873, Ben Horrell murdered Juan Martínez, a constable. A Lincoln posse caught up with him, and he and another cowboy were killed. On December 20, 1873, a wedding dance was taking place in Lincoln. The wedding party included the bride and groom, friends and relatives and half the population of the town,

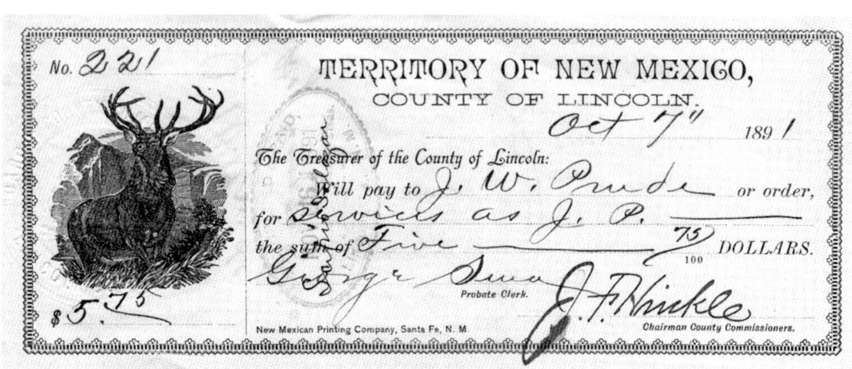
No. 221

TERRITORY OF NEW MEXICO,

COUNTY OF LINCOLN.

Oct 7th 1891

The Treasurer of the County of Lincoln:

Will pay to J. W. Prude or order,

for Services as J. P.

the sum of Five 75/100 DOLLARS.

Probate Clerk.

J. F. Hinkle

Chairman County Commissioners.

$5.75

New Mexican Printing Company, Santa Fe, N. M.

James J. Dolan formed a partnership to establish the Rio Feliz Land and Cattle Company. His half-interest in the Murphy Dolan mercantile store in Lincoln plus government contracts at Fort Sumner helped establish a chokehold and monopoly on area residents. *Author's collection.*

who were all Hispanic Natives. Everyone was having fun and dancing to the Spanish music that was being played by several area musicians. The Horrell brothers and their gang showed up, firing their pistols throughout the town, and then they attacked the unarmed wedding party. Here the story changes depending on who is writing it. The newlyweds were killed, along with other family members. Several others were left dead or wounded. The Horrell rampage of murder continued. They attacked Hispanic freight trains near Roswell, New Mexico, and in other areas. It is not known how many were killed before they escaped back into Texas, leaving a trail of blood behind them. This racial violence is known as the Horrell War.

Dolan and Murphy set up a very lucrative business in Lincoln that was called The House. They secured government contracts from nearby Fort Stanton. The story is murky, but apparently material, food and provisions distributed to Indian tribes ran through a well-manipulated group of individuals and red tape. This included beef contracts and cowboys who also served as hired guns for protection against others who might contest their claims. Tom Catron and his Santa Fe Ring of government officials, judges, lawyers and lawmen/outlaws provided a meandering set of links in what was believed to be an unbreakable chain. It came to the point that murders were not investigated, crimes went unpunished and no one faced the consequences of their actions. Indians received rancid worm-filled flour, stale bread and rat-infested or cockroach-filled food. Natives were dispensable. Mysteriously, items meant for Indians also showed up at mercantile stores run by men who infiltrated the system for their own purposes throughout the New Mexico Territory. Then Henry H. Tunstall entered the competitive fray. He came from a rich family in England with many connections. He also succeeded in acquiring land and cattle. The problem was, he also decided to set up his own mercantile business. For security, Tunstall hired his own cowboy/gunmen. The most famous was William H. Bonney, aka Billy the Kid. Tunstall was murdered because he and his men were a threat to The House. La Placita del Rio Bonito erupted in the great Lincoln County War, and the rest is history.

Just before this famous or infamous episode in New Mexico history, French American and Canadian fur traders, trappers and others were enjoying careers in a booming business up in Taos. They sought out beaver skins for the popular trade back east in beaver hats and other furs used for coats and other paraphernalia. Some, such as Christopher "Kit" Carson, married young Hispanic girls because they could inherit wealth and Spanish or Mexican granted lands they came by as heirs. They discriminately sought

This is an example of what became prevalent in New Mexico after opportunists and land grabbers flowed in. Land and cattle companies spread up everywhere, including the Milne and Bush Land and Cattle Company in Roswell. *Author's collection.*

out well-to-do families with only daughters who would inherit everything. Fur trapper Lucien Bonaparte Maxwell was about twenty-six years old at the time he married thirteen-year-old María de la Luz Beaubien. The only problem encountered was she had an older brother named Narciso who was first in line in inheritance of extensive lands and holdings. He died mysteriously. Maxwell stepped right in and claimed everything. He laid claim to a much larger area than what had originally been bequeathed in the original land grant. He had the land surveyed in northern New Mexico and into southern Colorado. His surveyors didn't consider Indian settlements or Hispanic communities located on those lands. The entire area then became known as the Maxwell Land Grant, as Lucien called it. He had discovered that a railway system would run into certain areas, so he immediately laid claims to those lands as part of the original grant.

The Maxwell Land Grant and Railway Company sprang up, rapidly grew and was supported by the Santa Fe Ring. Since the United States government passed the Homestead Act and similar legislation, and squatters also had their rights, this grew into a problem for Maxwell. Indian tribes and Hispanic residents were dispossessed of their lands with the help of troops from nearby Fort Union. Anytime a crime was committed, they said it was either Mexicans or Indians who did it. Lucien Maxwell was instrumental in founding the towns of Cimarron and Maxwell. He exploited all the resources of the vast area, including water, game, agriculture and mineral. From the forests, Lucien provided wood for railroad ties. Gold was also discovered on the land. In Maxwell and other nearby towns, there were saloons, hotels, brothels and gambling houses. Anything and everything that could provide fun and entertainment for railroad workers and miners was available. Maxwell and his proteges were all in for fun and profit. But there

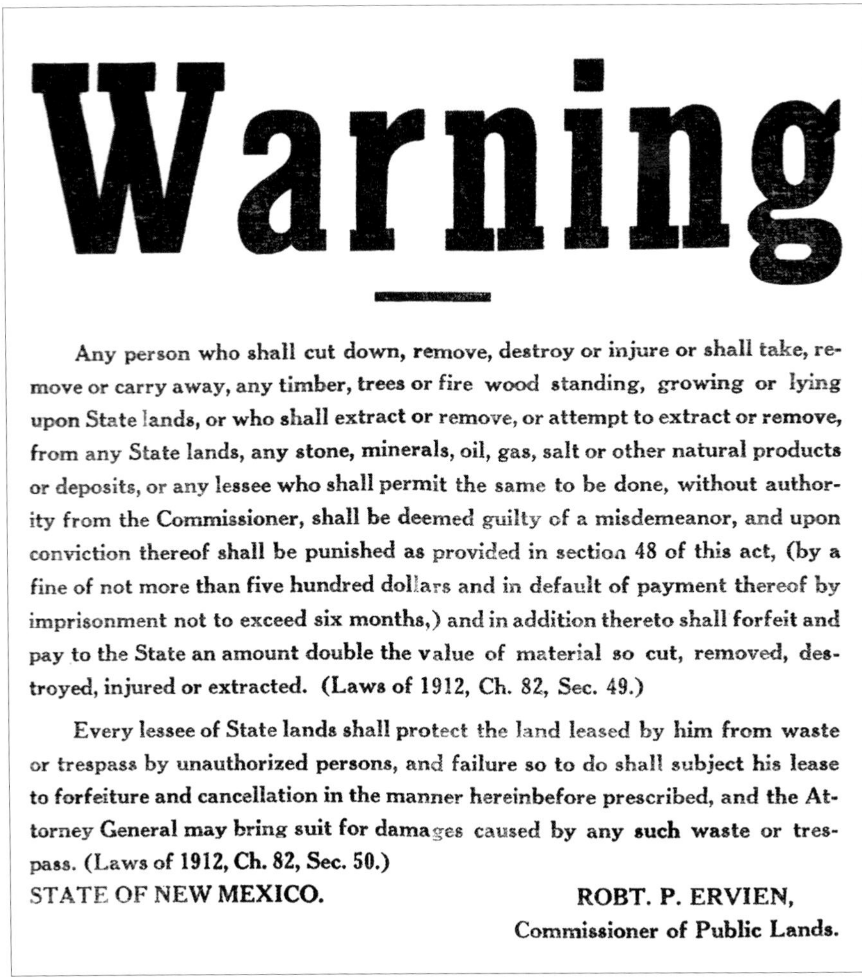

Warning

Any person who shall cut down, remove, destroy or injure or shall take, remove or carry away, any timber, trees or fire wood standing, growing or lying upon State lands, or who shall extract or remove, or attempt to extract or remove, from any State lands, any stone, minerals, oil, gas, salt or other natural products or deposits, or any lessee who shall permit the same to be done, without authority from the Commissioner, shall be deemed guilty of a misdemeanor, and upon conviction thereof shall be punished as provided in section 48 of this act, (by a fine of not more than five hundred dollars and in default of payment thereof by imprisonment not to exceed six months,) and in addition thereto shall forfeit and pay to the State an amount double the value of material so cut, removed, destroyed, injured or extracted. (Laws of 1912, Ch. 82, Sec. 49.)

Every lessee of State lands shall protect the land leased by him from waste or trespass by unauthorized persons, and failure so to do shall subject his lease to forfeiture and cancellation in the manner hereinbefore prescribed, and the Attorney General may bring suit for damages caused by any such waste or trespass. (Laws of 1912, Ch. 82, Sec. 50.)

STATE OF NEW MEXICO.

ROBT. P. ERVIEN,
Commissioner of Public Lands.

New Mexico common lands, which placed no restrictions on forest, water or other resources, suddenly came under total prohibited use. Razor-sharp barbed wire with different points and blades was strung up. Fencing could cut human flesh or severely injure wildlife. When New Mexico entered statehood in 1912, warning signs appeared everywhere. People were arrested and jailed even for minor offenses. *Author's collection.*

was a gold rush. Even placer gold was found. New miners arrived without Maxwell's blessing, and more people were squatting and submitting papers for homesteading. He complained to the authorities that these new arrivals were busying themselves by capitalizing on his hard work, investments and lands. By 1875, conflict and violence had erupted in the Colfax County War. Maxwell and his family moved to the abandoned military post of Fort

Sumner, and he set up camp there. His son Pete would see the killing of Billy the Kid by Sheriff Patrick Floyd Garrett in 1881 at his home.

An English group of investors purchased the Maxwell Land Grant and unknowingly fell into Lucien B. Maxwell's well-laid-out plan. The very well-financed group adapted quickly. They hired more gunmen who were directed to burn down homesteads and squatter homes and torch grasslands. During what became a reign of terror, cattle rustling increased, and freight wagons and stagecoaches traveling on the Santa Fe Trail (which ran through miles of the property) were attacked and robbed. Farther south from Cimarron, the town of Las Vegas became the "Wildest of the Wild West," as popular writer Howard Bryan put it. Lynchings were common at the bridge over the Gallinas River that separated East and West Las Vegas. Frequent hangings also took place at a windmill over a community well at the center of a large park in what was later called Old Town. Bat Masterson and Clay Allison took part in the war, and in Las Vegas, Doc Holliday and other well-known gunmen showed up to see what all the ruckus was about. There was a system of power and control led by none other than the Santa Fe Ring. Law-abiding citizens were not only threatened but terrorized. All civil rights were taken away, and there was no justice in New Mexico. The homesteaders, squatters, miners and those who supported them were outgunned by the English syndicate. When everything was at a brutal deadlock, the English group sold out to a Dutch faction. More than two hundred people had already been killed, of course, not counting Indian and Hispanic men, women and children. The number also did not include lynchings and murders that took place on the grant lands.

The federal government sued the Maxwell Land Grant and Railway Company Dutch owners because they were also laying claims to public domain lands in Colorado. The plea was sent to the United States Supreme Court. The Supreme Court justices concurred with the Dutch owners, saying, "We are entirely satisfied that the Grant, as confirmed by the Action of Congress, is a valid grant, that the survey and patent issued upon it are entirely free from any fraud."

This involved approximately two million acres of land in northern New Mexico and southern Colorado that successfully caused the physical displacement of an entire people and communities plus removal of their rights. Thomas Benton Catron and the Santa Fe Ring also accomplished getting millions of acres more.

What is left out about land interests and most often fraudulent claims in New Mexico is that burials, cemeteries, churches and chapels were deeply

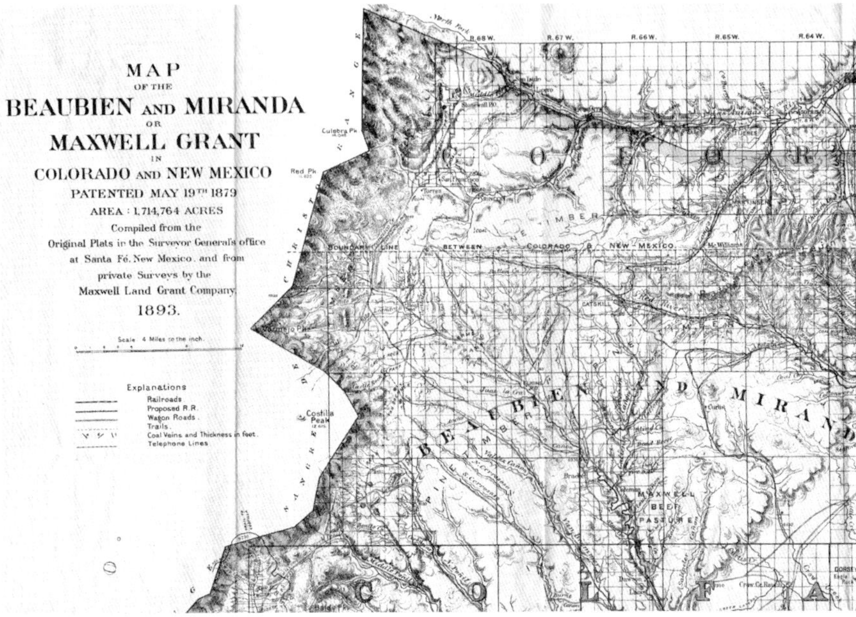

Maxwell Land Grant map, surveys, multiple homestead deeds and false documents were used to secure and affirm a land grant through the U.S. Congress that took in ancient Indian settlements and old Hispanic communities in millions of acres across northern New Mexico and southern Colorado. Countless people were displaced. *Author's collection.*

involved. People in those days buried loved ones with gold and precious stone jewelry, silver and other prized possessions. Grave robbers infiltrated burials and cemeteries. Indian and Hispanic patrimony was also pilfered and plundered. Indian artifacts made their way into private and museum collections. The folk art of Hispanic villages—such as painted and carved religious images in the round, referred to as santos, and flat panels called retablos—grew in popularity, value and demand. Some pieces of Indian and New Mexico artifacts sold for thousands of dollars in legal and illegal markets. Faithful Hispanic Roman Catholics often donated acres of land, homes and buildings and artistic items such as valuable paintings and sculptures to the Archdiocese of Santa Fe. Archbishop Lamy began the practice of selling off the lands and whatever else was donated for profit.

Land speculation continued into the turn of the twentieth century. Some people were victimized by those claiming to own lands they had no rights to. The promise of a new life in a new territory where all freedoms were honored was a powerful magnet. Free and available land claims had the unequaled ability to attract people even to the most desolate areas. Black people from the South were trying to escape the terror of the Ku Klux Klan, torture, lynchings and death. Many fled to other areas, including New Mexico. Some staked homestead claims in an area fifteen miles south of Roswell. Eventually, a self-sustaining community was established, called Blackdom, New Mexico. The total combined acreage of all the Black homesteaders was fifteen thousand acres. There was a school, hotel, Baptist church, weekly newspaper and community center where people sang and danced to music provided by local singers and musicians. They also had farming and livestock. An annual Juneteenth celebration took place in Blackdom. This event commemorated the date on June,19, 1865, when 250,000 slaves were finally freed in neighboring Texas. "Justice delayed, Justice denied," was a cry heard throughout Texas. Anti-Black violence was an unknown in New Mexico Territory. In fact, under the Spanish and Mexican governments, Blacks and Native Americans were automatic citizens with all the rights and privileges provided for all citizens. During the American Civil War, New Mexico volunteers fought the Confederacy to protect the Union and won a major victory at the Battle of Glorieta that has been called the "Gettysburg of the West." The primary focus of the battle was to keep New Mexico from becoming a slave state. The Texas Republic fought for slavery up to the bitter end. New Mexico, in contrast, was against slavery. Juneteenth in Blackdom was celebrated with prayer

Stock certificates were sold at a premium on nonexistent mines or mines located on Indian lands or Spanish and Mexican land grants. Many were fraudulent claims including sketchy ownership. *Author's collection.*

Civil rights activist Dolores Huerta served as the parade grand marshal for the Fourth of July Fiestas in Las Vegas, New Mexico, in 2018. She is pictured with Ralph Arellanes at the Old Town Park during the festivities. *Photo by Marcella Arellanes.*

meetings, the singing of spirituals, Black family gatherings and a large festival to which surrounding residents were invited. Blackdom resident Lucy Henderson wrote, "Here the Black man has an equal with the White man, here you are reckoned at the value which you place upon yourself. Your future is on your hands."

Blackdom Townsite Company was organized, and Blackdom Oil Company was established once oil was discovered on the lands. Oil leases were then being sold to bring in additional revenue for the community and residents. Water was provided for farming and homes through artesian wells. Eventually, those wells dried up. Water was trucked in, but that was too costly. The town was in its death throes when a severe drought and dust bowl hit the area. Some tried to hold on, but most families relocated to other cities such as Roswell and Albuquerque. Descendants of the early families of Blackdom continued to receive oil royalties for generations. They also participated in protest marches and demonstrations in Albuquerque, and pastors in Baptist churches in New Mexico also spoke out against discrimination during the national racial tensions of the 1960s.

Chapter 3

VOICES CRYING IN THE WILDERNESS

When Padre Luis Demecio Jaramillo delivered his sermons in various churches of New Mexico, he never minced any words. The congregation would sit up and take notice. At the pews, many squirmed, while others sat in shock and awe.

> *The pulpit is a special place* mi gente [my people]. *From this pulpit one should be relevant to what is going on in New Mexico and the world and not turn a blind eye. Are you all blind! Stepping on toes and making people feel uncomfortable is my job. If you leave here from this church thinking and acting, then I will have succeeded in doing God's work.*

Father Jaramillo was born in Springer, New Mexico, in September 1931. He credited his birthplace and his mother as major influences in his life. His family struggled through hard work and kept a close relationship with the rest of the community.

Springer was named after Frank Springer, who had an interesting history. He became intensely interested in the fossils discovered by the loggers and workers who were cutting down hundreds of trees to fashion into railroad ties on lands owned by Lucien B. Maxwell. Frank Springer amassed one of the largest collections of fossils in the world, gathered from the lands situated on the Maxwell Land Grant. He sold some and donated the rest to the Smithsonian Institution in Washington, D.C., thereby sealing his prominence as a noted paleontologist and entrepreneur in New Mexico

The Reverend Father Luis Jaramillo was an outspoken member of the Alianza Federal de Mercedes spearheaded by Tijerina. Jaramillo preached on land theft and social injustice in New Mexico as a parish priest. At the pulpit, he prodded people to action and fight hard for civil rights. *Author's collection.*

history. Springer also served as the attorney for Maxwell, a fur trader, originally stationed in Taos, New Mexico, during the very lucrative fur trade that attracted many traders from Missouri. Eventually, Maxwell managed to lay claim to what he called the Maxwell Land Grant in northern New Mexico. Original Hispanic property owners and communities in the area contested his claims to the Bureau of Private Land Claims in Santa Fe and the New Mexico surveyor general. The bureau became notorious for sometimes taking up to fifty years to reach a decision, and it was required that all documents were to be presented in English to be considered valid during this time. This was in New Mexico Territory, where all official documents were written in Spanish, and all publications including territorial government legislative documents were also in Spanish.

Frank Springer brought the case of Maxwell's ownership of the land grant to the United States Supreme Court in Washington, D.C. The Supreme Court rendered a decision in favor of Lucien B. Maxwell, granting him title to 1,000,714 acres in northern New Mexico and Colorado. This became the Maxwell Land Grant Company. It is now known that fraudulent or forged documents were at times used to present land claims by American immigrants to New Mexico in court. At other times, original Spanish or Mexican land titles conveniently disappeared or were purposely destroyed. A territorial governor is noted as having used extremely valuable Spanish colonial and Mexican period documents stored at the Palace of the Governors in Santa Fe to light fires in the fireplaces. Lucien B. Maxwell's rise to power and fame would factor significantly in northern New Mexico history. He was an influential member of the notorious Santa Fe Ring, a group of unethical judges, lawyers, merchants and lawmen who became enormously wealthy by stealing millions of acres of land, water resources and cattle in New Mexico.

Frank Springer, in league with Maxwell, helped him set up the Maxwell Land Grant and Railway Company. The company capitalized on mining

The train station in Springer, New Mexico, circa 1884. Land opportunists maneuvered to steal thousands of acres from rightful owners to gain wealth by selling rights-of-way and railroad ties. This also included stolen cattle, horses and other foodstuffs for railroad construction. *Author's collection.*

coal on the lands, necessary for the trains, logging, ranching and all irrigation and water rights. Maxwell, as president of his company, also sold land leases to the government, which saw it much easier to deal with one person than an entire group of people. Railroad executives also realized the advantages to this. Maxwell hired cowboys and guns to uproot people from their homes. In fact, lands of the Taos Pueblo Indians were taken by the federal government in 1861. Around one thousand Taos Pueblo Indians were uprooted and placed in a remote area by Union troops.

Father Luis Demecio Jaramillo's family was one of the displaced Hispanic families that fell victim to Lucien B. Maxwell and Frank Springer. Most families fell into poverty and struggled to survive after they lost their farms and ranchlands. Father Jaramillo never forgot and stressed in his sermons, "A culture with roots is a culture that can bloom. A culture without roots only has plastic flowers. Now we only have plastic roots because we were uprooted from our lands and our ways of life. We need to do something about this right here and right now!"

Father Jaramillo was recognized as the spiritual leader of the civil rights movement of New Mexico. He had an interest in the life and times of Padre Don Antonio José Martínez of Taos. After studying Padre Martínez and the role he played in civil rights for the people in New Mexico, Jaramillo left New Mexico and entered the seminary and studied for the priesthood. After he was ordained, Father Luis received a JCL degree in canon law and taught at Howard University in Washington, D.C., and Malcolm X University in Chicago. Then Padre Luis Jaramillo returned to New Mexico to serve in his native land. He began to advocate for the marginalized in society. Father Jaramillo cofounded La Academia de la Nueva Raza (the Academy of the New Race), a cooperative researching land titles in New Mexico. This cooperative issued a publication called *La Resolana* to enlighten the public about land grant issues. He became the chaplain of the Albuquerque Black Berets, a group from the community of the Barelas area with the sole purpose of helping the poor and fighting against discrimination. Padre Luis, as he was affectionally called. proclaimed, "Justice here on Earth is fundamental to a spiritual path." He participated in the Poor People's Campaign in 1968 and served as vice chancellor of the Archdiocese of Santa Fe and chaplain of the New Mexico state legislature. He continued pleading on behalf of the poor with his authority and influence until he died at the age of eighty-nine.

Another leader and strong supporter of Hispanic causes and New Mexico Hispanic history was Dr. Henry J. Casso. He was a very humble man, as he pushed others along. He never sought recognition nor fought for it. He simply felt he was in the background putting a bug into people's ears and rejoiced when his actions bore fruit. His health and other obstacles he encountered along the way were merely hills meant to be crossed over to get to the next one. Henry J. Casso reminded everyone, "Sometimes we might stumble to try to go through one door, but eventually you will get to where you are going even if a door is slammed into your face."

He was always very animated, whether in phone conversations or in person. He gave life to whatever subject he took on. Lengthy discourse was always interspersed with a subtle joke and laughter. With a bright gleam in his eye, this social justice gladiator saw the seriousness of the situation for Hispanics not only in New Mexico but across the country.

This renowned civil rights advocate from New Mexico said he was whipped into shape as a young boy in an orphanage. He recalled, "It was at an orphanage where I learned to fight hunger and poverty. Other boys were bigger than me, so I not only learned to defend myself, but speak up. Boy, did I speak up!"

Perseverance led him to receive a doctorate in education at the University of Massachusetts. There, Casso helped create the first Massachusetts

Anxiety, acrylic on canvas, painting by Ray John de Aragón. The artwork depicts destruction of the environment and world amid carelessness and abuse. *New Mexico Highlands University Collections*.

Undergraduate Teacher Training Bilingual Program. He became a civil rights advocate at the height of the Chicano movement and was directly involved in President Lyndon B. Johnson's War on Poverty in the 1960s. Dr. Casso was determined to help eradicate poverty and improve the lives of Latinos across the country. A staggering dropout rate among Hispanic youth, high teen pregnancy and the loss of hope among the youth were his concerns. "We should never give up," he would say. "The siesta is over; we have to resort to action now…as high achievers, movers, and shakers."

Among his many deeds of service, Dr. Casso was the founder of the San Antonio, Texas Don Bosco Youth Center. As a priest, he created an organization called PADRES (Padres Asociados Para Derechos Religiosos, Educativos y Sociales, or Associated Priests for Religious, Educational and Social Rights). This was a national organization of Latino bishops and leaders of the Roman Catholic Church meant to spread awareness of poverty across the country. There, he served as the vicar for urban affairs and executive secretary of the National Bishops Committee for the Spanish Speaking. Back in New Mexico, Dr. Casso was a University of New Mexico professor and founding president of the National Institute for Professional Development and Project Uplift to prepare high school minority students for high-technology careers. The Albuquerque project spread to Texas, Colorado and across New Mexico, serving ninety thousand middle and high school students in the region. While attempting to fight discrimination against Mexican Americans across all levels, Dr. Casso became a founding board member of MALDEF (the Mexican American Legal Defense and Educational Fund). He assisted thirty-four students in becoming practicing attorneys. Then the accolades for Dr. Casso poured in. He was recognized as a Latino Legend in 2008 by AT&T. He received the New Mexico LULAC Medal of Honor. It is written that the distinguished Dr. Casso appeared in three hundred live TV programs and was recognized by the director general of UNESCO. He was also honored by the presidents of Mexico and Costa Rica.

Through his very notable work, Dr. Henry J. Casso attempted to lift all Hispanics to their rightful place in United States history. He, like Father Luis Jaramillo and many other notable people in New Mexico history, also fought vehemently for the national recognition of New Mexico's folk hero priest, Padre Don Antonio José Martínez. Dr. Casso was outraged at this oversight and held several Padre Martínez institutes and seminars to attempt to correct the historical record. I was included as a speaker and scholar on Padre Martínez. Dr. Casso promoted a documentary film on Padre Martínez and pointed out that the priest had the first law school for Hispanics in the 1830s, wherein he taught U.S. Mexican and Spanish law to his students. Some of his former students became the first successful Hispanic lawyers and judges in this country. Dr. Casso sought to bring out the truth about Padre Martínez and point him out as a major historical figure in U.S. history who strongly influenced our people to succeed in the nineteenth century. During the last years of Dr. Henry J. Casso's life, he devoted his time and energy to the recognition of Padre Don Antonio José Martínez of Taos while still espousing for help against the chronic and pressing needs of the poor and advocating for Hispanic education.

PART II

ENDLESS DIMENSIONS OF POVERTY

Chapter 1

MOVEMENTS FOR JUSTICE

Movements for democracy began rising almost immediately after New Mexico officially became a territory of the United States in 1848. A major point of contention if New Mexico were admitted as a part of the Union was whether it would become a slave state. This was an issue that was bitterly contested both in New Mexico and in Washington, D.C.

Civil Rights and Justice: The Force of Reies López Tijerina

The decade of the 1960s was marked by racial and social unrest, the Vietnam War, protests, tension and cultural chaos. Heroic national social justice and civil rights leaders such as Dr. Martin Luther King Jr., Cesar Chávez and Reies López Tijerina emerged and led movements directed toward human rights, human dignity and equal justice. Inspired youth took up the standards of civil rights, and their voices reverberated in the streets and across the nation. Out of the struggles and ashes of human despair, Reies López Tijerina rose up, took up the torch and vibrantly animated the scene not only in New Mexico but throughout the Southwest and the nation. Hispanic youth were caught up in the fervor and zeal of this remarkable period in New Mexico state and national history. *El Tigre* (King Tiger, as Tijerina was called) spoke out:

> *My motto is justice. Every time I think about my people it brings me to tears.* Lagrimas *stream down my face. They run like a river when I see the faces of anguish and hopelessness across Nuevo México and America. Join me today. Join La Alianza. Only an alliance of our people can see that justice is done. It is our right. Our Spanish language, our way of life and our land must be protected. You are the heirs of this beautiful land; your sons and daughters are the heirs.* Queremos Justicia.... *We want justice! Not welfare and powdered milk! We have had enough!* ¡Nuevo México está llorando, *New Mexico is crying!*

Reies López Tijerina was born in a farming community near Falls City, Texas, on September 21, 1926. His father was nearly crippled from working out in the fields. His mother died when Tijerina was six years old. His family had scraped out a living as itinerant farmworkers. Survival was through hard labor and sharecropping. Even children were involved in peonage, working for very wealthy ranchers and farmers. Tijerina and his siblings, all very young children, moved on as migrant farmworkers, along with countless others, after his mother died. Like many other children of these migrants, Reies and his siblings were self-taught. Texas, like other former Confederate states during those days, was extremely unfriendly and racist toward Blacks and the Mexican immigrant community but needed these workers to do the hard labor that others would not do. "No Mexicans Allowed" signs were strewn around many areas. Neither Mexican migrants nor any other Hispanics could go into some restaurants or live in "Whites Only" residential areas, and they were restricted under the penalty of the law from anything that only Anglos could take part in, including drinking water from race-exclusive water fountains. Anyone breaking regulations was incarcerated for breaking harsh rules and laws by prejudiced juries and racist court systems.

Tijerina, at the age of seventeen, had the opportunity of attending the Assembly of God Bible School in Saspamco, Texas. He attended for three years and was an exemplary student, receiving praise and honors in his classes. At twenty, Tijerina went on to do missionary work in the southwestern United States and became highly recognized for his zeal and preaching. The young preacher tried to construct churches and communities in Texas, Arizona and California during the 1950s, but his buildings were destroyed and burned. He was often beaten and brutalized. This made the fiery preacher more determined not only to stand up for his people who lived under poverty and abuse under horrific conditions

Reyes López Tijerina, at an Alianza meeting, explains member participation in the Poor People's March in Washington. *Author's collection.*

but also to be their apostle, seeking justice. He bought law books and intensely studied them for self-protection and to protect his congregation of loyal followers.

The popular preacher's first contact with New Mexico was in Santa Fe around 1947–49, enjoying not only the climate and scenery but also the friendliness and openness of the locals. They all communicated quite easily in Spanish, since New Mexicans in general were quite adept in the Spanish language. The young preacher in his late twenties traveled around meeting and shaking hands with the people, especially old-timers who had a wealth of knowledge about land loss. Tijerina traveled freely from one state to another. He was in New Mexico's Chama Valley in 1950. He also traveled to Tierra Amarilla during the same year. This northern New Mexico community would make a lasting imprint on Tijerina that would influence the rest of his life and career. In 1954, he published a book in Spanish called *Hallara Fe En La Tierra*, loosely translated as *Will Faith Be in the Land?*

Reies Tijerina went on a ceaseless quest for knowledge about land theft in New Mexico. He traveled to Santa Fe to study ancient documents he found in the state archives. He became an expert in reading the difficult Spanish colonial records he found. He also went to Mexico and Spain and researched there. The more Tijerina discovered, the more he wanted to find out. He learned about La Alianza Hispana Americana, a group that had been very active in early Las Vegas, New Mexico. He also researched Los Obreros, a labor union that had been a large group in northern New Mexico who had sought to effect changes in working and social conditions and government for the betterment of Hispanics. Tijerina was especially attracted to the legacy of Las Gorras Blancas, an organization of ranchers and farmers based in San Miguel County and other northern counties. At one time, there were around five thousand members who sought civil rights and equal justice between 1870 and the late 1890s.

During the Civil War in New Mexico, close to twelve thousand Hispanic ranchers and farmers volunteered to fight for the Union. They provided their own arms, horses and provisions. Hundreds died fighting Confederate forces that invaded and took over the territorial capital in Santa Fe. Troops under Lieutenant Colonel Manuel Antonio Chávez succeeded in defeating the Confederates at the famous Battle of Glorieta. After the end of the war, former Confederate officers, soldiers and southern sympathizers arrived in New Mexico en masse and meticulously sought to control the government and steal lands in cahoots with land swindlers and thieves who were infiltrating Indian lands and the rest of the country.

Not only was property stolen, but people were also uprooted from their homes and dispossessed of personal belongings, and some were indiscriminately murdered if they did not leave. The U.S. government also freely took over millions of acres of Indian lands and ancient Spanish land grants. Many of these lands then were leased to immigrant white ranchers, shady enterprises and dubious politicians. Leases ran up to ninety-nine years at pennies on the dollar. A law was passed that mercantile stores would handle burials only in designated areas. Corners in stores often kept bodies waiting to be buried. Before this, deaths in families were a family affair with people constructing homemade coffins and handling anything and everything related to caring for their deceased. Now it turned into a very lucrative enterprise for shady merchants who became rich. Grievances had fallen on deaf ears in the courts, so it was felt that the only recourse to protect people's rights was by striking back. However, the result was failure.

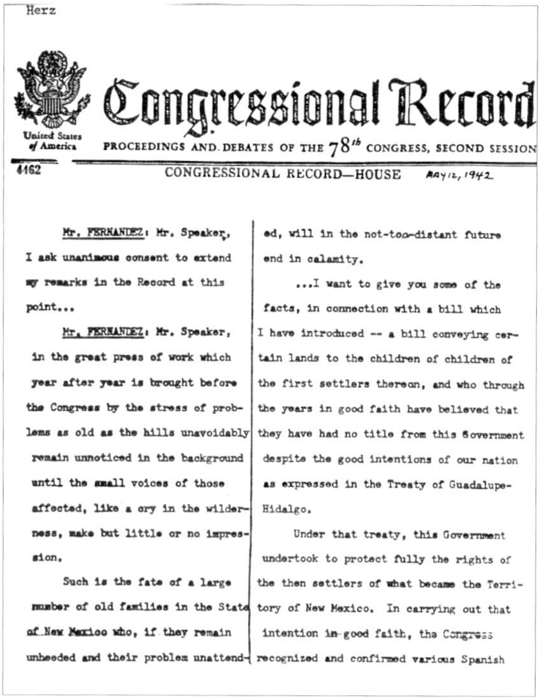

Herz

Congressional Record

United States of America

PROCEEDINGS AND DEBATES OF THE 78th CONGRESS, SECOND SESSION

4162 CONGRESSIONAL RECORD—HOUSE May 12, 1942

Mr. FERNANDEZ: Mr. Speaker, I ask unanimous consent to extend my remarks in the Record at this point...

Mr. FERNANDEZ: Mr. Speaker, in the great press of work which year after year is brought before the Congress by the stress of problems as old as the hills unavoidably remain unnoticed in the background until the small voices of those affected, like a cry in the wilderness, make but little or no impression.

Such is the fate of a large number of old families in the State of New Mexico who, if they remain unheeded and their problem unattended, will in the not-too-distant future end in calamity.

...I want to give you some of the facts, in connection with a bill which I have introduced -- a bill conveying certain lands to the children of children of the first settlers thereon, and who through the years in good faith have believed that they have had no title from this Government despite the good intentions of our nation as expressed in the Treaty of Guadalupe-Hidalgo.

Under that treaty, this Government undertook to protect fully the rights of the then settlers of what became the Territory of New Mexico. In carrying out that intention in good faith, the Congress recognized and confirmed various Spanish

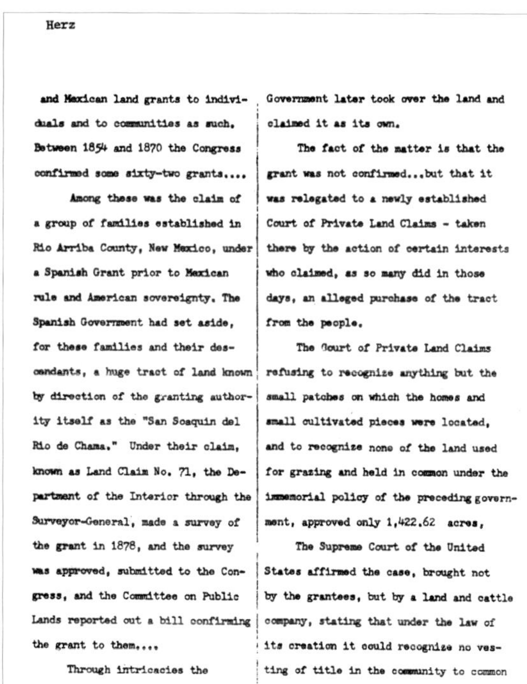

Herz

and Mexican land grants to individuals and to communities as such. Between 1854 and 1870 the Congress confirmed some sixty-two grants....

Among these was the claim of a group of families established in Rio Arriba County, New Mexico, under a Spanish Grant prior to Mexican rule and American sovereignty. The Spanish Government had set aside, for these families and their descendants, a huge tract of land known by direction of the granting authority itself as the "San Soaquin del Rio de Chama." Under their claim, known as Land Claim No. 71, the Department of the Interior through the Surveyor-General, made a survey of the grant in 1878, and the survey was approved, submitted to the Congress, and the Committee on Public Lands reported out a bill confirming the grant to them....

Through intricacies the Government later took over the land and claimed it as its own.

The fact of the matter is that the grant was not confirmed...but that it was relegated to a newly established Court of Private Land Claims - taken there by the action of certain interests who claimed, as so many did in those days, an alleged purchase of the tract from the people.

The Court of Private Land Claims refusing to recognize anything but the small patches on which the homes and small cultivated pieces were located, and to recognize none of the land used for grazing and held in common under the immemorial policy of the preceding government, approved only 1,422.62 acres.

The Supreme Court of the United States affirmed the case, brought not by the grantees, but by a land and cattle company, stating that under the law of its creation it could recognize no vesting of title in the community to common

Top: Antonio M. Fernández, who served in the U.S. Congress from New Mexico from 1943 to 1956, lobbied in the Seventy-Eighth Congress on land issues affecting impoverished Hispanics and Indians. *Author's collection.*

Bottom: Reverse of Congressional Record with the appeal to Congress by New Mexico Congressman Antonio M. Fernández asking for an investigation into land grant problems. *Author's collection.*

Eventually, people in New Mexico had enough. Poverty among Hispanics was rampant. Educational opportunities were minimal. Many turned a deaf ear to the plight of grievances of the generation's old loss of lands. Reies Lopez Tijerina, fighting for human rights, felt he could make a difference. His words were filled with heartfelt emotion. His magnetic personality and charisma attracted many not only to his profound cause but also to hear and reflect on his very passionate words:

> *The Hispano people of Nuevo Mexico had the fire before I began the Alianza. La lumbre, the fire that burned in their hearts and souls erupted from a hundred years or more of suffering. It was a long history of pain and suffering in the valleys which were bathed in tears. Medrado Abeyta united the heirs of the Merced of Tierra Amarilla, a very old community land-grant.*
>
> *He was the one who got Congressman Antonio Fernández, to present the claims of the San Joaquín Grant to the United State Congress. The land had been stolen by the federal government and turned over to the Forest Service. They in turn granted leases to the land to wealthy businessmen and ranchers for ninety-nine years. These corrupt men put up barbed wire fences closed off the lands and kept the original residents out with rifles and guns. These rapacious men were also protected by the Forest Rangers. People were kept out by force and could no longer get firewood, nor water their livestock or fish on the rivers that everyone shared and held in common.*
>
> *There were many old people when I first got to Tierra Amarilla, Tecolote, Mora, many places, even Santa Fe. They all gave me their stories about outsiders coming in and taking everything. They cried and I cried with them. Tears streamed down their old faces, and I felt their deep pain. They talked to me about the old days when there were beet fields in Las Vegas, when there was plenty of water, and they had chickens and sheep. It was a good life they said, but land thieves' hardships, and taxes they couldn't pay, ended all of that. It was the first time I heard someone say, "They stole our land, and gave us powdered milk."*
>
> *Poverty was everywhere. The old ones died, and their sons and daughters and then later grandsons and granddaughters took up the struggle to get their lands back. All these stories inspired me to write my book,* Mi Lucha por la Tierra, My Struggle for the Land. *I started La Alianza Federal de las Mercedes, the Alliance of Federal Land Grants. My movement began with a handful and grew in New Mexico to thousands of members. It became strong, very strong and scared a lot of people. Politicians, government officials, and the wealthy that capitalized on massive land frauds ran scared of me and the Alianza.*

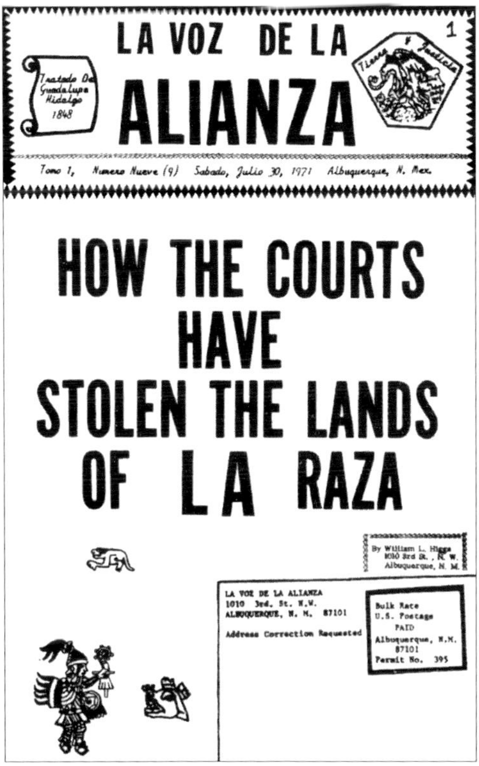

LA VOZ DE LA ALIANZA 1

Tratado De Guadalupe Hidalgo 1848

Tierra y Justicia

Tomo 1, Numero Nueve (9) Sabado, Julio 30, 1971 Albuquerque, N. Mex.

HOW THE COURTS HAVE STOLEN THE LANDS OF LA RAZA

By William L. Higgs
1010 3rd St., N.W.
Albuquerque, N. M.

LA VOZ DE LA ALIANZA
1010 3rd. St. N.W.
ALBUQUERQUE, N. M. 87101

Address Correction Requested

Bulk Rate
U.S. Postage
PAID
Albuquerque, N.M.
87101
Permit No. 395

Left: *La Voz de la Alianza* (the *Voice of the Alliance*). Tijerina's periodical kept members informed as to the land grant organizations' movements and progress. *Author's collection.*

Below: New Mexico Army National Guard troop movements during the Tierra Amarilla Courthouse Raid on June 5, 1967. Alianza land grant activists protested land theft in New Mexico. *Unknown photographer, courtesy New Mexico Historical Society.*

The Tierra Amarilla Courthouse Raid, which took place on June 7, 1967, in New Mexico, made national and international news for various reasons. News flashes included descriptions of a revolt against the government by those allied with communism and communist leaders such as Fidel Castro of Cuba and Che Guevara, one of his military favorites. Media manipulation included reports of an armed revolt taking place, especially after shots were fired. The New Mexico Army National Guard was activated, and the New Mexico Air National Guard was placed on standby. What began as a peaceful protest by residents and those interested in the issue of lost lands and social justice in an isolated and virtually unknown community rapidly grew out of proportion. Armored tanks rolled into the area, and armed troops in military vehicles stormed in. Men, women and children were arrested and placed under guard in fenced livestock pens. Although some aspects of the so-called raid remain murky up to this day, other details emerge.

Rio Arriba County district attorney Alfonso Sánchez had been previously informed that there would be a very large gathering of New Mexico protestors from throughout New Mexico, possibly numbering in the hundreds, overrunning the county seat and the peaceful town of Rio Arriba. This was instigated by radical Reies López Tijerina, some people claimed. The gossip that was spread grew and frightened the district attorney to the point of seeking assistance from the local sheriff. He was apparently advised that the sheriff's department would not be able to control this massive, rowdy crowd because Tijerina had thousands of followers in New Mexico. It is said the county district attorney traveled to the state capital at Santa Fe and consulted with state officials, including Lieutenant Governor E. Lee Frances. Governor Dave Cargo was out of state attending the National Governor's Conference in Michigan. It was determined that the planned gathering should be prevented.

The district attorney was provided with the disposal of the New Mexico State Police. Other law enforcement agencies also participated. Roadblocks in and out of Rio Arriba were set up, and they were also placed in some distant areas. Armed security checkpoints checked drivers' licenses, and anyone attempting to go in and out of Rio Arriba town and county had to state their purpose of being there. Anyone deemed suspicious was taken in for further questioning. As was to be expected, tensions ran high. An all-points bulletin was supposedly issued for Alianza leader Reies López Tijerina, who had been effectively calling for a social justice protest rally to take place in Rio Arriba. When he was informed

Friday Morning, June 9, 1967

Brother Anselmo Arrested

Reies Tijerina, Aides Still Elude Officers

State police late Thursday arrested Anselmo Tijerina, 47, at his home in Hernandez, but his brother, Reies Lopez Tijerina, 40-year-old land claim insurrectionist leader, and three aides continued to defy capture.

In another move, federal authorities here were checking into a purported threat Reies Tijerina reportedly made against families of U.S. and state officials in a news release mailed to Albuquerque.

Anselmo Tijerina was taken to Santa Fe for arraignment on charges filed after the shooting raid last Monday on the Tierra Amarilla Courthouse by the Reies Tijerina - led claimants to thousands of acres of land grants in the Southwest. Two officers were shot and seriously wounded and two persons were kidnapped during the raid.

Related Stories D-1, G-10

Officers continued their search for Reies Tijerina in Albuquerque but the other three were believed to be hiding out in Rio Arriba County where Anselmo Tijerina was arrested.

The three are Cristobal Tijerina, another of the leader's brothers, Balthazar Martinez and Moises Morales.

16 Persons Charged

Altogether 16 persons were charged in connection with the courthouse raid. The warrants accused the insurrectionists with two counts of kidnaping and three counts of assault with intent to commit a felony.

State Patrolman Nick Saiz, shot during the raid, remained in critical condition at Bataan Methodist Hospital. The other wounded officer, Sheriff's Deputy Eulogio Salazar, also shot, was reported in satisfactory condition in a Santa Fe Hospital.

Meanwhile, Jack Love assistant U.S. attorney here, said his office is "studying" for possible federal law violation in the news release bearing Reies Tijerina's signature.

Mailed from Espanola

The news release was mailed from Espanola Wednesday and received Thursday by the Associated Press and United Press International bureaus in Albuquerque.

The *Albuquerque Journal* of June 9, 1967, reported the arrest of Anselmo Tijerina and the search for Alianza leader Reies López Tijerina after the Tierra Amarilla Courthouse Raid, which received national and international media attention. *Author's collection.*

about what was happening, he and other Alianza leadership believed their right of assembly was not only being infringed on but their civil rights were being denied. They decided a citizen's arrest of the district attorney was warranted. It was also believed District Attorney Sánchez held an ingrained animosity toward the Alianza movement and its organization. Sánchez ordered the arrest of Tijerina, a member of his family and others. Tijerina's brother Cristóbal and a couple of other Alianza members were placed in the county jail. When a few Alianza participants went to serve their citizen's arrest on Sánchez, he had been forewarned and immediately left. Then the situation at the courthouse went out of control when those jailed were released by the Alianza participants. A physical altercation ensued; a sheriff's deputy drew his pistol, and others present also had firearms. Several injuries resulted. Eulogio Salazar, the Rio Arriba County jailor, escaped the turbulent scene through a nearby window and headed for the hills, running for his life. He then hid for days. Sometime later, the jailor was found shot to death. No one was tried or convicted.

What was taking place behind the scenes is not entirely clear but remains a mystery in need of solving. FBI director J. Edgar Hoover was investigating Dr. Martin Luther King Jr., United Farmworkers Union President Cesar Chávez, Alianza leader Reies López Tijerina and apparently Malcom X. These civil rights leaders were having a vast effect on the social conscience of the nation and needed to be stopped, according to what certain individuals firmly believed. In New Mexico, United States Senator Joseph Montoya spoke out against Tijerina and his movement. Martial law was declared, and all protest gatherings were strictly prohibited. An arrest warrant was issued for the influential Reies López Tijerina, who had an exceptional ability to secure the loyalty and devotion of many New Mexico Hispanics. The largest manhunt in New Mexico history then took place. This extensive and organized search included different sheriff departments throughout the state, the New Mexico State Police, military police and the Federal Bureau of Investigation. After the massive manhunt, which included all New Mexico law enforcement agencies, Tijerina was finally captured. He vehemently protested his innocence. The land grant leader claimed he was on his way to Tierra Amarilla but never got there. After a lengthy trial, Tijerina was found innocent of all charges that were leveled against him, but his career was severely blemished. However, the turbulent scene at the Tierra Amarilla Courthouse proclaimed Tijerina as a grand hero renowned for his courage, great strength and daring in the national Chicano movement taking place in other states.

After the highly touted Tierra Amarilla Courthouse Raid on June 5, 1967, a massive manhunt took place that crossed into Mexico. The search was for land grant leader Reies López Tijerina. He was finally captured and arrested. *Courtesy Adelita Medina.*

Reies López Tijerina was not prone to staying quiet. Next, he wanted to help the descendants of the San Joaquín del Rio Chama community land grant regain their land. This area, located in the county of Tierra Amarilla, had been taken over by the federal government and turned into a national forest. A protest took place at the Echo Amphitheater Campground located on the federal reserve on October 13, 1969. Tijerina's wife, Patsy, attempted to light a forest sign on fire. She was unsuccessful but was arrested by a forest ranger. Details were also murky during this incident. Reies López Tijerina was arrested for vandalism and destruction of federal property in a national forest. He was tried and convicted of this and sentenced to a two-year term by Federal Judge Eloy Sutin. Tijerina eventually wound up at the maximum-security La Tuna Federal Detention Center in La Tuna, Texas. He was at times placed in solitary confinement, supposedly for his own well-being. Tijerina began to suffer from severe

ALBUQUERQUE JOURNAL

(T. M. PEPPERDAY, publisher, 1926-1966, H. P. PICKRELL, editor 1926-1964)

An Independent Newspaper

Published At Seventh St. and Silver Ave. SW, Albuquerque, New Mexico By The Journal Publishing Co.

Robert A. Brown, Editor John McMillion, Executive Editor

A-4 Thursday, June, 6, 1968

A Stunned Nation

The shooting of Sen Robert F. Kennedy has stunned the nation into shocked disbelief that it could happen — again.

President Johnson spoke for all Americans when he said: "There are no words equal to the horror of this tragedy. All America prays for his country, and for Kennedy's recovery."

There is bitter irony in the fact that Kennedy — member of a family oft beset by tragedies — disdained security in his quest for the nation's highest office.

Throughout his campaign—with far less protection than that given his brother, President John F. Kennedy, on that dark November in Dallas — Senator Kennedy plunged into frenzied, screaming crowds seeking to grab and tug at him.

He seemed to believe he had to prove that he could move more freely and with more confidence among the throngs than could President Johnson.

Marchers Pray, Tijerina Argues In Washington

WASHINGTON (AP)—The marchers in the Poor People's Campaign, whose own leader was killed two months ago, prayed Wednesday for the recovery of Sen. Robert F. Kennedy and for an end "to this national sickness before it engulfs America in catastrophe and death."

The prayer was led by the Rev. Ralph David Abernathy, who succeeded the slain Dr. Martin Luther King Jr. as head of the Southern Christian Leadership oCnference and its march on Washington. The marchers met in front of the Lincoln Memorial.

"Hear our prayer and heal this man," they prayed. "Let him come out of his bed of sickness and back into life."

THE DAY brought another squabble between the Negro leaders of the campaign and Reies Tijerina, head of a group of Spanish-Americans from New Mexico who are claiming land rights under ancient Spanish grants.

Tijerina had scheduled a march to the State Department to discuss the southwest land question and was incensed to find campaign leaders ignoring it and planning the prayer session.

Seizing a bullhorn over which Hosea Williams, director of demonstrations, had just announced the plans, Tijerina accused Williams of running out on the Mexican Americans.

He challenged Williams' leadership and said it was threatenng to break up the coalition of Negroes, Indians and Mexican - Americans that was one of the strengths of the campaign.

"THEY WANT to run everything for the Black brothers and we will not stand for it," Tijerina said later to newsmen.

Asked whether he would take his group out of the campaign, he said, "That's up to them," meaning the SCLC leaders.

Tijerina and about a dozen followers went to the State Department where they learned Secretary Dean Rusk would be unable to see them because he was meeting with the visiting president of Costa Rica.

"Who comes first, foreigners or Americans?" shouted an angry Tijerina as he led his little band away.

Effect Numbing

Presses Stop As Kennedy Tragedy Hits

By BOB BROWN

The headline "Robert Kennedy Shot at California Rally" hit many Albuquerque residents Wednesday morning like an unexpected arctic blast.

Many turned cold inside as they flipped their Journal open after picking it up from the lawn. Others stared, speechless, murmuring "Oh, God, not again."

The effect was numbing on those who had gone peacefully to bed long before the tragic happenings of the early morning hours.

They had no way of knowing that television and radio announcers had spent the pre-dawn hours reviewing and re-reviewing the dramatic Los Angeles events. They simply had no way of knowing that in the quiet, peaceful night events were once again taking place . . . events destined to shock the world.

THE JOURNAL, of course, had no desire to be this instrument of shock. The aim of its staff was to bring as much news as possible to its subscribers despite production problems. After all, the Journal had already gone to press with its Four-star edition, the one which is delivered to Albuquerque homes. Other editions were already on their way to points across the state.

The year 1968 was a pivotal one that saw the assassinations of Dr. Martin Luther King Jr. and Robert Kennedy, the Poor People's March and the activism of Tijerina, the Alianza and the Black Berets. *Author's collection.*

depression and delusions. As recommended by psychiatrists, Tijerina was then transferred to the Springfield, Missouri Medical Center for Federal Prisoners of the Criminally Insane.

Father Luis Demecio Jaramillo, the chaplain of the South Valley Black Berets, a group of Chicano activists, expounded, "Some people need to get slapped before they wise up and take notice. Learn and do what is right! Do what bothers the hell out of people, make them think and make changes for the good of everyone!"

Father Jaramillo, a Springer native, did not hold back in his Catholic church sermons—nearly always speaking in Spanish when he needed to make a stronger point. He supported Tijerina as well as other members of the clergy who fought for civil rights in New Mexico. Before a protest march from Las Vegas to Santa Fe, Tijerina proclaimed:

> *We have just started to write a new page in the history of Nuevo México. We need actions not words! The time is right for us to get rid of our fears.*

ALBUQUERQUE JOURNAL

(T. M. PEPPERDAY, publisher, 1926-1956, H. P. PICKRELL, editor 1926-1964)

An Independent Newspaper

Published At Seventh St. and Silver Ave. SW, Albuquerque, New Mexico
By The Journal Publishing Co.

Robert A. Brown, Editor John McMillion, Executive Editor

A-4 Saturday, June 8, 1968

Report Tijerina Has Quit March Is Denied Here

Reports that land grant leader Reies Tijerina has deserted the Poor People's March in Washington were denied at a press conference here Friday.

Father Luis Jaramillo, who returned Tuesday night from Washington, said Tijerina left Washington "to be with his red brothers in Oklahoma," but was due to return to Washington Friday.

Jaramillo also had this to say:

"Distortions by the press and news media have clouded the real issues of the campaign and destroyed the true meaning and purpose of the poor people's march on Washington," Jaramillo said.

Present at the conference were Shirley Hall Witt, a campaign coordinator, and delegates Bernie Armijo and Katherine Hattenbach. All recently returned from Washington.

Jaramillo also said there was no controversy between the Mexican-American contingent in Washington and the predominantly-Negro Southern Christian Leadership Conference.

The delegates also denied that members of Tijerina's Alianza are being trained in guerrilla warfare by outsiders from Mexico. The charge was made by Santa Fe Dist. Atty. Alfonso Sanchez.

Father Jaramillo said additional funds are being sought to send another bus to Washington and replenish the New Mexico contingent in Washington.

Kennedy Memorial Vesper Scheduled

A special Memorial Vesper Service for Sen. Robert F. Kennedy will be held at Messiah Lutheran Church, 11515 Lomas NE, at 7 p.m. Sunday.

"Do Not Boast About Tomorrow," a phrase from the twenty-seventh chapter of the Old Testament book of Proverbs will be the sermon theme of the Rev. Eugene Gauerke, pastor of the local congregation.

"My God, What's Happening to America" will be the sermon

Washington Merry-Go-Round

By DREW PEARSON
And JACK ANDERSON

WASHINGTON—August 2 has been set for the adjournment of Congress, and this time there's a pretty good prospect of meeting that deadline.

Reasons are:

1. The national conventions of both the Republican and Democratic parties take place in August.

2. The Poor People's march has descended on Washington, and most Congressmen want to get out of town before trouble starts.

They figure that when the heat boils down on Resurrection City there is bound to be violence.

ORDINARILY IT'S the southern solons who are delighted to remain in Washington all summer. It's just as hot back home as it is in the nation's capital, and their air-cooled offices here are fairly comfortable. But this year the prospect of delegations from the "poor people" bombarding Congress has spurred increased congressional activity for adjournment.

It may well be that the August 2 deadline will be met.

While Poor People's marchers were storming government offices and breaking Supreme Court windows in order to get better laws for themselves, the insurance lobby sneaked through the Senate a better law for itself in the guise of helping the poor.

Both the insurance companies and the poor people used the same tactics—a sit-down by the former, sit-ins by the latter.

C-4

Leader of Poor March June 19 Quits in Dispute

WASHINGTON (UPI) — Bayard Rustin quit Friday as director of the mass Poor People's March through Washington June 19 because of a dispute with leaders of Resurrection City over the goals and tactics of their campaign.

The Rev. Ralph David Abernathy accepted Rustin's resignation with regrets for what he called "very minor differences" and said Sterling Tucker, executive director of the Washington Urban League, had been asked to take over the job.

The June 19 march had been regarded as the most dramatic—if not the climactic—public demonstration of the month-old Poor People's March for more jobs, housing and welfare assistance. Whether it can now succeed without the organizational genius of Rustin, the gray-haired theoretician of the Civil Rights movement, was questionable.

Rustin, head of the A. Philip Randolph Institute in New York, organized the 1963 civil rights march on Washington that drew 210,000 persons. Tucker, little known outside Washington, was praised by Abernathy as a "staunch supporter" of the Poor People's March as coordinator of its

Albuquerque Journal newspaper stories of June 8, 1968, centered on the famous Poor People's March slated to take place in Washington, D.C. Father Luis Jaramillo served as the spokesman for the Alianza. Tijerina collaborated with Reverend Abernathy on New Mexico participation. *Author's collection.*

> *They have stolen our land! Our lifeblood is* la tierra, *the agonizing land that runs through our veins is shedding tears!* ¡Vamos adelante! *Let's go forward and move Nuevo México to its best, and in doing so, the rest of our country! With this, we will help everyone in our beloved nation!*

Civil rights attorney William "Bill" Higgs joined Tijerina in his honorable quest for equal justice. Higgs had received national attention in the media for representing James Howard Meredith, a Black student who was denied enrollment at Ole Miss in Jackson, Mississippi. This was a flashpoint in the national civil rights movements across the country. Many took up the standard of desegregation across the nation, including Rosa Parks, who refused to sit in a Blacks-only section of a public bus. Bill and I hit it off immediately, and we became close friends. It was he who invited me to attend Tijerina's meetings and speeches. I was thrilled. At the Alianza

June 8, 1968 ALBUQUERQUE JOURNAL

Treaty Complied With, Says Official

Tijerina Claims Discounted in Capital

WASHINGTON (UPI) — The State Department said Friday that all provisions of the 1848 Treaty of Guadalupe - Hidalgo with Mexico have been complied with in every respect. Land grant leader Reies Tijerina claims his people were "robbed" of lands in violation of the treaty.

State. Dept. Press Secretary Robert J. McCloskey said Tijerina's group, which claims millions of acres of land in the Southwest were "robbed" from them in violation of the treaty, should take their case to the courts or seek congressional action rather than press the issue with Secretary of State Dean Rusk.

However, he said, Rusk would be available to see the group—in Washington with the Poor Peoples March—some time next week if a mutually agreeable time could be arranged.

THE BAND of some 25 New Mexico residents of Mexican ancestry led by Tijerina tried earlier this week to meet with Rusk but he was busy with other appointments.

McCloskey said both the U. S. and Mexico had fulfilled their obligations under the 1848 Treaty of Guadalupe-Hidalgo, which ended the Mexican War, ever since the treaty was signed. He said the Mexican government had never advised the United States regarding any failure to carry out all its obligations.

The group, led by Tijerina, as near as the State Department can conclude, has challenged the U. S. government on three points:

—**THE TREATY** is invalid because it was signed by an unauthorized individual.

—It guaranteed corporate, political and judicial rights for a separate sovereign state in the Southwest.

—That certain Mexican-Americans were deprived of the property rights guaranteed under the treaty.

In response to the first point, McCloskey said the State Department has "no evidence that the treaty was defectively concluded." He pointed out that both governments proclaimed it in force July 4, 1848.

AS FOR A sovereign state in the Southwest, McCloskey pointed out that the legal terms of the treaty provided the United States Constitution would apply to all of the territory transferred to the United States and this automatically would preclude the existence of sovereign entities within the territory.

With regard to the third point, concerning property rights, State Department officials pointed out that disputes involving such rights have been considered by the U.S. government many times, have been handled by U.S. courts, have been the subject of Congressional legislation, and were considered by a special claims commission Congress established at the end of the 19th Century.

Therefore, they said, the Dept. of Justice rather than the Dept. of State would be the appropriate executive agency to consider the validity of any of these claims.

THE MEXICAN government has never raised the question. Thus, any individual who feels he has been denied justice in the previous considerations should take his case to court or seek special legislation.

As a matter of historical record, the treaty actually was signed on Feb. 2, 1848, by a State Dept. representative who had exceeded his powers because he had already received orders recalling him.

The orders came from President Polk.

Polk fired the official, Nicholas P. Trist, for his disobedience but the President found the terms of the treaty so much to his liking that he sent it to the Senate, which ratified it March 10, 1848.

The question of Trist's authority to sign the treaty was never brought into question by the Mexican government, since it ratified and accepted the terms after the Senate action here.

The *Albuquerque Journal* of June 8, 1968, carried a report that the U.S. State Department saw no merit in New Mexico land grant activist Reies López Tijerina's contention that the United States government broke the Treaty of Guadalupe Hidalgo, which ended the Mexican-American War in 1848. *Author's collection.*

headquarters, we gathered to make plans for conferences and marches, such as the Poor People's March on Washington, D.C., where Tijerina met with Native American and Black leaders such as the Reverend Jesse L. Jackson of the National Rainbow Coalition, Malcolm X and the Reverend Ralph Abernathy.

Cesar Chávez, addressing Alianza members at the headquarters on Third Street in Albuquerque, said, "*Yo soy uno de ustedes.* I am one of you in the struggle for equality, for human rights and dignity. It is the struggle of all of us." Chavez's last words stayed resonating in our ears: "*Me han dicho muchas veces que no se puede hacer. Que no podemos cambiar las cosas. Yo les digo, sí, se puede hacer. Podemos cambiar la injusticia. ¡Sí se puede!* (They have told me many times that it cannot be done. That we cannot change things. I tell you, yes, it can be done!) *¡Yo estoy con ustedes!* (I am with you!)"

Words like this, during this time and place, led us all to action. As teenagers and young adults, we were bent on action making changes for the betterment of all those who were downtrodden in American society. Native Americans had a movement. Black Americans had their movement. Hispanics had El

Movimiento, calling for parity, equality, equal justice, respect and dignity in New Mexico and in the American mainstream. However, circumstances and destiny had other unexpected plans in an event that drew worldwide attention that led to strange and rapid horrendous results. On June 15, 1967, many people from throughout New Mexico gathered peacefully at Tierra Amarilla, New Mexico.

It was a nice day in northern New Mexico, bright and sunny. Close friends and families gathered to listen to Reies Tijerina expound on racial injustices in New Mexico and America. People hugged and shared stories, and everyone spoke about past injustices in New Mexico, about lost lands and the mistreatment received by the corrupt judicial system of the past. All gathered for music and danced to New Mexico Spanish music, as well as enjoyed a huge potluck at the town center. This very significant day in New Mexico left a lasting and enduring mark on New Mexico state and national history. What began as a peaceful gathering to hear the words about injustice spoken by the great Tijerina grew and spread into violence that was spurred on and spread by political officials and police officers bent on prohibiting any protest, no matter how peaceful, against historic corruption and injustice in New Mexico. Chief among these officials, according to what is written and available to the public, was Rio Arriba County district attorney Alfonso Sánchez. It is believed he arbitrarily issued orders suppressing peaceful protests and peaceful gatherings. Governor David F. Cargo had left the state for other business, and New Mexico Lieutenant Governor E. Lee Francis was in charge. Although Cargo, as governor, was the commander-in-chief of the New Mexico Army National Guard and the New Mexico Air Force National Guard, he was apparently unaware of what would take place.

In American history, U.S. citizens have always had the right to perform a citizen's arrest when someone is committing a crime such as burglary; rape; destruction of public property; causing violence; or harming, injuring or killing someone. Reies López Tijerina had spent many hours studying the law. He firmly believed American citizens had inalienable rights to protect themselves in their persons, in their property and their possessions. So when Tijerina believed crimes had taken place in New Mexico history and were taking place in the present, he could not turn away; he firmly believed he needed to step in. Tijerina very quickly made it onto the national stage.

No one knew what was happening behind the scenes politically in New Mexico. As was happening throughout the country with all civil rights leaders—especially the Social Justice Triad of Dr. Martin Luther King Jr., Cesar Estrada Chávez and Reies López Tijerina—all were considered

THE HIGHLANDS **CANDLE**

Volume 46, Number 2 — *Las Vegas, New Mexico* — Friday, October 15, 1971

Tijerina Welcomed At Highlands

Reies Lopez Tijerina speaks before a crowded gym. (Photo by CORDOVA)

Reies delivers message of justice

On October 12, Reies Lopez Tijerina spoke before a crowd of more than 2000 students, adults and children at Stu Clark Gym.

After serving two and a half years in prison, Reies has finally been given the opportunity to express his message through channels which were never open to him before.

Today he is being welcomed by the same pepple who five years ago were putting him down. The news media responsible for much of the hostilities toward Reies, has now allowed at least unbiased reports on his release from prison his present movement for justice.

On that night Tijerina shared his message and plea for justice with his audience. He emphasized the fact that we have been misinterpreting the meaning of justice when we let a uniform, a badge and a gun represent justice in this country. 'Justice", he went on to say, 'is an emotion, a feeling which can be promoted just like love or hate. If ss something which has to be developed, encouraged, revolutionized popularized.

To Tijerina it seems incongruous that people spend so much money exposing and promoting sex--'Why can't more money be used in promoting and exposing justice?" Reies implored. If Sex is not love, neither can the law be justice. His main concern is that we as a People join hands in making justice a reality for all people not only for those who can afford to buy it.

Mr. Ray de Aragon
Activities Vice President
Student Senate

At the annual El Día de la Raza event held at NMHU on October 12, 1971, Reies Tijerina delivered one of his famous speeches, which called on university students to stand up on the principles of equal justice for themselves and their families. The powerful orator traveled throughout the country delivering his speeches at events, universities and colleges. *Author's collection.*

enemies of the state and were targeted for eradication by the government by whatever means available. Dr. King was arrested twenty-nine times for civil disobedience. Chávez was arrested for leading national boycotts against farming conglomerates that controlled immigrant workers with low salaries and horrendous working conditions, including threats and forced labor. Chávez led pickets, protests and marches against unjust practices that were not allowed by federal law. He was arrested along with three thousand followers and put in jail. Chávez had served valiantly during World War II in the armed forces and followed the premise of nonviolent resistance pioneered by India's Mahatma Gandhi, an anti-British colonialism nationalist who led a movement against British rule. He staged hunger strikes and was assassinated on January 30, 1948. Gandhi inspired political movements of civil rights and freedom all over the world. Cesar Chávez in California followed Gandhi's leadership by also engaging in hunger strikes. One eventually led to his death.

Dr. King was assassinated on April 4, 1968. There were plots to kill Chávez and Tijerina. Alianza headquarters was bombed in Albuquerque. FBI Director J. Edgar Hoover and his agents kept files on all three civil rights leaders. Tijerina was ordered to turn over his membership files to the FBI and New Mexico officials, which included the phone numbers, addresses and personal information of around five thousand New Mexico citizens. Tijerina refused to do so. As it happened, two FBI special agents came to my home in Albuquerque and questioned me for two hours about my own affiliation with the Alianza. They left, satisfied that I had been away at an out-of-state Air National Guard training when the event at Tierra Amarilla took place.

One might ask the following question: What was the immortal legacy of the extreme activism of Reies López Tijerina? Many have failed to recognize how this civil rights leader affected the history of New Mexico and the United States. Tijerina was a champion of education, especially higher education. He often spoke about the lack of Hispanic leadership and faculty positions in colleges and universities across the country. In

In 1968, I kept a calendar on which I marked important dates on Alianza de las Mercedes meetings, conferences and gatherings. It turned out that 1968 impacted American history in many ways. Dr. Martin Luther King Jr. and U.S. Senator Robert Kennedy, who was in the midst of a campaign for president, both were assassinated. The land grant organization founded by Tijerina was also impacting communities in the Southwest. *Author's collection.*

Graham's Selection Ignites Ire Of Some HU Student Factions

By STEVE MAY
Editor

Members of certain student groups on the Highlands campus were scheduled to continue today their boycott of classes in protest of what they term "discrimination" in the selection of the new HU president.

Amid cries of "Viva La Raza" and "Aragon for President," members of the Chicano student population and others conducted a protest rally Wednesday to show their disapproval of Dr. Charles J. Graham as the choice for the presidential post.

The dissenting groups, who were supporting Dr. John Aragon of the University of New Mexico for the top administrative seat here, charged the HU Board of Regents were discriminatory in the selection. Protest leaders claim the regents did not give Aragon, who is a graduate of Highlands and now director of the UNM Cultural Awareness Center, fair consideration for the post.

An estimated 300-400 students turned out for the noon-day rally and heard speakers laud Aragon and condemn Graham. The main gripe offered by protesters was that Graham did not know the problems confronting Northeastern New Mexico. Leaders pointed out that Aragon, having grown up in this area and attended Highlands, knew the problems and how to meet them.

Speakers included Francisco Gonzales, president pro tem of the HU student senate; District Attorney Donald Martinez; Reies Lopez Tijerina Jr., Albert Amador, a member of the State Board of Education, and Arsenio Gonzales, a former state legislator.

The protest rally did not stay in front of the Student Memorial Center. Leaders organized a march to the Old Town Plaza and back up National Street to

An editorial covering the selection of Dr. Frank Angel at Highlands was carried locally and nationally. Listed in the editorial was the name of Donaldo "Tiny" Martínez, San Miguel County district attorney. Martínez strongly supported Tijerina, as well as many other politically powerful individuals from northern New Mexico, such as Fidel "Chief" Gonzales and West Las Vegas Mayor Junio López. *Author's collection.*

School is back to what might be termed "normalicy" after the serious incident that arose at Stu Clark Gym last Monday at mid-morning.

"I don't know what happened, it all seems pretty suspicious to me. I think they should all be suspended, all of them, they were faking," commented Highlands Police Officer Jim Baca.

Meanwhile the **Candle** has learned that the two professors instrumental in removing many of the HU students from the scene of the incident, Harry Lancaster and Bryon White are presently at home recovering from their ordeal. Both are expected to be back in their offices by next week.

Ray John de Aragon

Consolidation discussed

Governor David F. Cargo today announced that a merger between Highlands and the University of New Mexico is being considered.

Cargo said that the Board of Legislative finance has been considering combining the state's colleges and universities into two mega-versities. This would lower administrative costs and reduce duplication of effort between schools, while maintaining competition between the schools.

THE HIGHLANDS Chicano Power

SCANDLE

Volume 42, Number 17 *Las Vegas, New Mexico* *March 29, 1968 (Dist. Apr. 1, 1968)*

The name of the New Mexico Highlands University student newspaper, the *Highlands Candle*, was changed in an issue to the *Highlands Scandle* and was widely distributed during student demonstrations. *Author's collection.*

1970, a position for president opened at New Mexico Highlands University in Las Vegas, New Mexico. Many highly qualified Hispanics applied for the position, which had been held by white/Anglos since the institution's founding in the late nineteenth century. The student body at NMHU, composed primarily of Hispanic students from New Mexico, supported Dr. John Aragón, who had a distinguished career. Dr. Aragón was passed over by the board members, who instead hired Dr. Charles Graham from Wisconsin on May 22, 1970.

The students were outraged and were spurred on by Tijerina, who vocally encouraged them to make this a major issue in his fiery speeches. Protest marches took place, and posters, effigies and other material were posted on the campus. A student takeover of administration offices took place. Additional material was taken to what would have been Graham's home. The NMHU campus police and Las Vegas Police Department

LANDS CANDLE

Las Vegas, New Mexico — Friday, October 1, 1971

First Chicano President

DR. FRANK ANGEL

President Of HU Marks Milestone

After more than 200 years of struggling for social, political, economic and educational equality, the Chicano people are now beginning to see a realization of their dreams.

The appointment of Dr. Frank Angel as President of Highlands University is a milestone in the Chicano's struggle for recognition.

In an area with a high concentration of Spanish-surnamed people, there existed a need to have a University with a 'cosmopolitan' outlook, incorporating programs in Indian culture, Spanish culture, Black culture and related arts - educational programs that relate to bilingual students.

Chicanos felt that in order for this type of university to evolve, we would have to have a president at Highlands who would know New Mexico, understand the problems of our area, understand the minority groups of the Southwest, and who would have ideas about making education relevant to the Southwest minority groups.

For eighteen years, under the 'Donnelly Regime,' Highlands was viewed as an institution that had established itself as an ivory tower, ignoring community needs and offering no true relevance to minority students.

As Dr. Willie Sanchez has stated in the past, 'There was a lack of proper role models ... there seemed to be a ceiling above which the Chicano students could not rise. It's pretty difficult to convince a kid that there's a place for him in the world when there is nobody to look up to.'

Above: The *Highlands Candle* featured an announcement of Dr. Frank Ángel as the new president—the first Hispanic president of a university in the nation. *Author's collection.*

Opposite: An alumni publication called *Highlands Highlights* from New Mexico Highlands University listed the distinguished career of Dr. Frank Ángel. The new president began immediately in his new position, first by creating a division of Chicano Studies and then setting up a bilingual program. This new program in Spanish and English was a New Mexico groundbreaker, offering bachelor's and master's degrees in this area. Other accomplishments during his tenure are too numerous to mention. *Author's collection.*

Highlands Highlights

New Mexico Highlands University — Artes · Scientias · Humanitates — 1893

Vol. XXI, No. 4 | Las Vegas, New Mexico | July, 1972

Dr. Angel Installed At Formal Inauguration

Dr. Frank Angel, Jr. was formally installed as the twelfth president of New Mexico Highlands University on June 5, 1972.

The inaugural ceremonies were held in Ilfeld Auditorium and featured Sidney P. Marland, Jr., U.S. Commissioner of Education, as guest speaker. A banquet honoring Dr. Angel was held the previous evening.

Dr. Angel, who began his academic career over three decades ago, took over the presidential duties from acting president Dr. Ralph Carlisle Smith in September, 1971.

Born and reared in Las Vegas, Dr. Angel taught elementary grades in one- and two-room schools in San Miguel County from 1932-37. He then taught in the Nambe Experimental Community School until 1941. During the years 1941-45, Dr. Angel was a B-24 bomber pilot in the Central Pacific, and achieved the rank of captain in the U.S. Air Force.

Upon his return to civilian life, he received a bachelor of science degree in elementary education from the University of New Mexico. He later became principal- supervisor for the Albuquerque Public School System, a position he held until 1950.

In 1950 Dr. Angel earned a master of science degree in education and sociology from the University of Wisconsin. Until 1954 he worked for the State Department of Education. In 1955 he received a Ph.D. in education administration from the University of California at Berkeley.

From 1955 until his appointment as HU president last fall, Dr. Angel was professor of educational administration, Department of Educational and Administrative Services at UNM.

BULLETIN:
**President Angel has announced that in case of any more bomb threats professors are to call in to Mr. Elliot's office in reference to obtaining another classroom.
Suitable space will be given.**

DR. FRANK ANGEL, JR.

Reies López Tijerina congratulates Dr. Frank Ángel after his appointment as president of New Mexico Highlands University in August 1971. *Author's collection.*

officers threatened the students with arrest. However, many students came from families with strong political influence. This helped pacify the situation, although some were still arrested. The result was that Graham declined the position. Chicano students, led by Tijerina, succeeded in having Dr. Frank Ángel, a Las Vegas native with close ties to New Mexico, hired as the new president in August 1971. At first glance, the hiring of Dr. Ángel would have caused only a ripple, but it quickly became a torrent of national news. Tijerina's involvement and speaking out on important issues relating to Latinos in education also helped the push for the hiring of Hispanics in universities and colleges as well as their being placed as department heads, college deans and other high posts.

This was not the only educational issue Reies López Tijerina spoke out publicly on. He wrote about and vocally related the history of public education in New Mexico:

> *How could Nuevo México go from one-room schools and teachers hired by communities and with children who not only learned English but mastered it? They used McGuffey's Readers in classrooms with children from all ages and grade levels. Many of these kids grew up to have important jobs and careers. There are children with not enough to eat! They have no shoes on their feet! And New Mexico politicians have thrown them out into the street!*

Tijerina railed against Mexican kids who spoke little or no English being placed automatically in special education classes because teachers who did not speak Spanish shunned these students. His cries for better education that would explore history and heritage were ignored. He claimed this was leading to a terrible crisis in our public schools. Tijerina strongly affirmed:

> *Cultural needs are ignored. Bilingual programs have failed. The poverty level has miserably increased. Kids are dropping out of school. There is hunger and misery everywhere that is ignored. When will they wake up to the needs of our people? Kids don't know how to read or write. When and how did this happen? Young children need to have a sense of pride and security to succeed. They need music, dance, arts and crafts. Racism has no part in our schools from teachers or principals. Children should not be led to be ashamed of their history, whether it's Indian, Spanish or Black. There is emphasis on sports; why not on learning for everyone?*

New Mexico Governor Jerry Apodaca with civil rights leader Reies López Tijerina at the New Mexico State Capitol building in Santa Fe. The New Mexico State Public Education Department building is named after Governor Apodaca. *Photographic Collection (#000-654-0098, CSRW, UNM Libraries).*

Martin Luther King Jr. said:

> *The ultimate measure of a man is not where he stands in moments of comfort and convenience, but where he stands at times of challenge and controversy. In ancient times, the ability to read separated the wealthy and the poor, the educated and the ignorant, the free and the enslaved. The theme of perseverance continues to be prominent among themes in many peoples' lives as they face adversity. These themes are even more explicit within the lives of those marginalized and facing injustice in both small and large ways each and every day.*

Chapter 2

MARCHES, PROTESTS AND RESISTANCE

"The Name of the Land Is Juan"

Behind the liberators was Juan
Working, fishing and struggling
In his carpentry or in his damp mine.
His hands have worked the land and measured
the roads.
His bones are everywhere.
But he lives. He returned from the land. He is born.
He has been born again like an eternal plant.
All the nights impurity tried to bury him.
And now, in the dawn, he speaks with lips that will not be sealed.
They bound him and now he is a staunch soldier.
They wounded him and now he blooms with health.
They cut off his hands and he strikes blows with them.
They buried him, and he comes singing with us.
Juan, yours is the doorway and the road.
The land is yours, my people,
the truth has been born with you,
from your blood.
They could not exterminate you....
—Pablo Neruda

It was snowing and bitterly cold. Winter winds blew across the hills and valleys of southern New Mexico. The extreme cold sent shivers across the women's spines. Frostbite nibbled at their feet. A large group of women had painstakingly gathered to support their husbands, brothers and grandfathers in a very powerful protest. It was not only speaking up and taking a stand but resentment against abuse, mistreatment and economic slander. It was Silver City, New Mexico, during the 1950s. The United States was just recovering from two major wars. World War II had just ended, with much joy and celebration. Recovery was just taking place from the Korean Conflict. Veterans from both returned to New Mexico seeking a new life for themselves and their families. What they encountered back home was loss of properties. Unpaid mortgages, drought and many issues and hardships affecting families through funding war efforts and vital support left their toll on New Mexico in particular and the United States in general. Life for people was hard.

Back home in New Mexico in the dead of winter, women who included young and old, mothers, grandmothers and daughters, spent hours working, drawing and inscribing flat pieces of wood and everything they could lay their hands on to bring up their cause. The lives of their families were in jeopardy. Their husbands and sons were working in dangerous conditions; some were dying. They had no running water, electricity or heating. They dug the ground for outhouses and had to provide their own drinking water and sources for cooking. The men could do nothing. So these women, wearing their long thick coats, cloths pulled tightly around their heads, babies crying and children tugging at their skirts, decided they would not give up. There was nothing left to do but carry signs that read, "Miners Walk, and Scabs Crawl." What they fashioned in pictures and words gained a great deal of attention locally and nationally. The women were arrested and thrown in jail along with their children. Their story was carried in *Life* magazine, *Newsweek* and the *New York Times*. The FBI investigated. What did this all mean?

Native Americans and Hispanics in New Mexico had been fighting for equality for so long it was disheartening. Historically, they had been denied their homes, mistreated and discriminated against, which was approved by the government and the courts. The public displays of protest were a result of a long history of suffering and despair for the women. They would not stand down and be a broken people. Their display of support for the United States in previous wars should have been enough for them to be heard.

A major episode that took place during World War II adversely affected Hispanic families. The majority of returning New Mexico veterans were

At the University of Albuquerque, the Southwest Cultural Center recognized civil rights activists from the Chicano, Black and Native American communities in New Mexico. *Author's collection.*

Hispanic. A whole unit had participated in the infamous Bataan Death March. The 200th Coast Artillery unit fighting in the Philippines was composed primarily of soldiers from New Mexico. The total number was 1,816. Most were fluent in Spanish, which was one of the main languages spoken on the Philippine Islands. Because of this, U.S. military commanders decided to deploy these troops to fight the Japanese forces there. American forces were defeated, and the troops were captured. These men faced torture and starvation, with many dying in a forced march to a Japanese prison camp. Some were bayoneted along the way. Only 829 survived. Some returning veterans spoke back home about seeing close friends being maimed and starved until they were skeletons and their bodies being dumped into pits along the way. Some were still alive when they were buried. Names of Bataan Death March survivors were often misspelled by record keepers or were omitted entirely, so families at times did not know what had happened to their loved ones who had fought in the Philippines. Others remained as prisoners of war for many years after the march. Some of the survivors had scars from brutal attacks over their entire bodies. Some said they were buried, and yet, they survived.

Of note is that very little is written about the Hispanic women who aided and supported the men who left New Mexico to serve their country during World War II. Empowerment for these brave and courageous females took the form as volunteers in the Women's Army Corps, the Women's Auxiliary Corps, the Army Nurse Corps and the Navy WAVES. Some risked their own lives by tending the wounded on the battlefield. On the homefront, many served as Rosie the Riveters, denim-clad, riveting airplanes needed on the battlefield. During the Korean War, a large factory was opened in Las Vegas, New Mexico, to produce military parachutes for the soldiers. This factory employed over three hundred women. They had learned how to sew at young ages, trained by their mothers and grandmothers and other female family members. They were used to hardship and pain. There was a very dramatic change from a mostly agrarian life in rural communities to an urban one with few jobs being available for both men and women. Then the unthinkable happened to the people and the land.

The Atomic Age also came by way of New Mexico. The world's first nuclear explosion took place within or near Socorro County on July 16, 1945. It was in an area that was called the Trinity Site. Los Alamos near Santa Fe was the center of labs, carrying out scientific experiments. Offices located in Santa Fe were a part of what would be referred to as the Manhattan Project. It was a government top-secret deal in the works, unknown to residents in New

Mexico, meant to detonate an atom bomb. Land formerly part of a Spanish land grant and land belonging to the Mescalero Apache was appropriated by eminent domain. This meant the lands and structures were expropriated by the government without compensation to the owners in a process called inverse condemnation. The treaty conditions between the United States and Mexico that ended the Mexican-American War concerning the guarantees of land rights were totally ignored and disregarded. About half a million people, mostly Hispanic and Indian, in a 2,700-square-mile area of New Mexico were affected by a nuclear test. Some lived 12 miles away and others within 150 miles of the detonation of an atom bomb. Crops, livestock, the land as a whole and all water resources were affected. The people were not warned to evacuate because the test was "top secret." J. Robert Oppenheimer, the lead scientist who created the atom bomb, was quoted as saying, "Now I become death, the destroyer of worlds."

These New Mexicans were apparently considered expendable. Contaminated ash fell from the sky for weeks. Cattle and horses had severe burns, and people exposed to downwind fallout experienced cancerous tumors, birth defects and stillbirth. A huge spike in infant deaths took place. Healthcare was unavailable or costly for those affected. These people ate contaminated vegetables, meat and fruit and drank contaminated water. There was emotional and financial distress and death that affected a large population of New Mexican families for generations. No one was eligible for compensation due to the nature of the secret government project. It was a scientific test to find out about the destruction that could be caused by an atomic explosion. This test was like the destruction of the Spanish town of Guernica to find out the effectiveness of the bombardment of a city and civilians by the Nazi German air force. Pablo Picasso was so incensed by this he created a masterpiece that stunned the world in his heartrending protest. After the nuclear test in New Mexico, two atomic bombs destroyed the cities of Hiroshima and Nagasaki in Japan. It was claimed this effectively ended World War II. New Mexico veterans returned to their homes. They found access to job opportunities were limited. The men and women who survived the nuclear test in New Mexico were also shunned when they sought work.

From 1950 to 1953, the United States was involved in the Korean War. New Mexican soldiers were deeply involved in this conflict that involved several countries. It is often called the "Unknown War" because, unlike World War II, this military engagement received little attention. Many of the Hispanic soldiers and veterans are also unknown. Nearly 200,000 Hispanics from the United States participated in this international engagement. Most of the men are listed as Mexican American, including those from New Mexico. The number of New Mexican casualties is unrecorded. What is acknowledged is that Hispanic soldiers received the highest number of decorations in the United States, including Bronze Stars, Purple Hearts and Medals of Honor. Once home, New Mexican Hispanic World War II and Korean veterans found very few job opportunities except for mining.

An ancient Spanish saying in New Mexico that expressed the sentiment of the Hispanic population in New Mexico was "*Mi casa es su casa.* (My home is your home.)" People were accepted with open arms. Outsiders visiting the communities were always welcomed to enter homes and were greeted graciously and provided with warm and delicious food and drink. Travelers going from one area to another often found lodging in strangers' homes and were provided anything they needed at no cost at any time of the year. It was a way of life in New Mexico, borne out of generations of sharing and giving. Those traveling into New Mexico and the federal government took the welcome signs literally. They capitalized on the land and its people, especially when it came to mining ventures led by the federal government. The United States government for the most part claimed it owned and controlled all mineral deposits in New Mexico. As the country became more involved in war efforts, copper and zinc mining became prevalent in the state. After the nuclear explosion at Trinity site, a uranium rush took place in New Mexico. It is very possible that when the world's first atomic bomb was built in Los Alamos, the uranium may have come from deposits located in the state.

The Grants uranium mining district, located west of Albuquerque, produced more uranium than any other area in the nation. It ranked in the top seven in the world. Both open pit and underground mines were located there. There were 1,100 uranium mines and millsites in New Mexico. Mining extraction and production was the state's leading industry. In the early 1950s, a company named Empire Zinc, a subsidiary of the New Jersey Zinc Company, secured leases from the government and land through manipulation on a vast area near Silver City, New Mexico, for zinc extraction and production. Zinc was used in paints, ointments, lotions such as calamine and cosmetics. Zinc was alloyed with copper and brass, and rolled zinc strips were used in dry batteries. Zinc was also used for coinage. Demand for zinc by the government increased substantially during World War II and the Korean War. The Santa Rita Copper Mine, also in southern New Mexico, produced massive amounts of copper for coinage and many other uses.

The United States government employed a system of rationing and limiting the purchasing of materials and goods deemed essential for the war. Oil was needed for airplanes, ships and tanks and to run factories. Therefore, gasoline was rationed. Tires and other rubber materials were also meant for military needs. From January 1, 1942, until July 1945, no new automobiles were produced. Metals were scarce, as were coffee and sugar. War ration books were printed with red and blue stamps based on a point system that was often confusing and continuously changing. Blue stamps were used for canned fruits, soups, juices and vegetables. Red stamps could be used for meats. Everything was based on supply and demand, regional and economic factors. Eastern and midwestern states had priority, while western states such as New Mexico were on the low end. Rationing was therefore based on allowance, and high prices were unregulated.

Supplying the military with materials and goods came first. Private companies obtained lucrative defense contracts. Businesses dealing in mining interests created a monopoly. These enterprises soon controlled and manipulated the U.S. economy. National defense mining became the leading industry in New Mexico. Hundreds of returning Hispanic war veterans found limited job opportunities, so they became miners to provide for their families. They worked under miserable conditions. They often worked deep underground in damp mines with little or no ventilation. At times, they used dynamite and were injured. Some died from their injuries. Zinc mining, for example, created an illness called metal fume fever, which led to genetic defects, organ damage and neurological problems. Zinc was also hazardous to the soil and surface waters. Copper mining harmed the skin, eyes and lungs. It destroyed crops and deteriorated the land. Uranium mining contributed to the emission of radiation and the release of radon, a radioactive gas that led to lung cancer. Copper, uranium and zinc mining became leading industries in New Mexico.

Empire Zinc owned and operated a large zinc mine in Grant County, New Mexico. Along with the mine, the company had extensive landholdings in the area, as well as properties in the town of Hanover. The nearest city was Silver City, approximately thirteen miles away. The company maintained a firm grip economically and socially in the region. The company also controlled the only access road into and out of the mining area, and 90 percent of all employees lived in the nearby town of Hanover on property owned by Empire Zinc, where they were separated according to employment status.

Empire Zinc had a three-tiered level of staff and employees. The administration, consisting of white workers, ran the operation at high pay.

Salt of the Earth photo shows the despair and impoverishment faced by people in New Mexico. Miners and families built shacks out of scraps. Ironically, zinc from mines was used to galvanize metal. The galvanized tub at left was used for bathing and other household chores. Pieces of galvanized sheets cover the crude house. *Author's collection.*

The executives operated out of offices on the surface. Residences were provided for the white contracted employees. The technical staff aided the executives and were also white employees. These were high-paid staff running the strict operation of the mine. These employees lived in furnished homes with utilities including indoor plumbing provided for themselves and their families. All underground workers were poorly paid Hispanic miners supervised by Anglo management. Anglo staff were under contract, whereas Hispanic miners were on hourly wages. Hispanic miners had the lowest pay and lived in miserable conditions. The miners had to rent from the company parcels of land on which they had to construct their own living quarters for themselves and their families. Building materials were not readily available, so scrap lumber and any usable items went into constructing their living quarters. Most were makeshift places to live with no running water, electricity or heating. Wood stoves they purchased provided heat in winter and cooking surfaces. The workers had to provide their own drinking water and sources for cooking. Water was brought in by tank trucks. They dug the ground for outhouses. Many children were unable to attend school. Those who could encountered prejudice in the schools because many could not speak English. Medical facilities were in Silver City, so illnesses of the miners and their families at times went untreated. The Empire Zinc strike, also known as the Salt of the Earth strike, took place due to the severe working conditions of the zinc miners and the poor living situations of their families.

Empire Zinc officials threatened the miners and their families with deportation to Mexico, although some were New Mexico Hispanic natives whose ancestors had been here since the sixteenth century or Mexicans born in the United States when they went on strike. The miners were threatened with suspension if they did not relent and return to work. Empire Zinc officials decided to close the mine to break the strike. However, miners working in other New Mexico mines joined in on the picket lines. When the miners continued the strike, Empire Zinc issued a blank statement saying the miners would be fired. The miners left the strike and were replaced by their wives and children, some of whom had already been actively involved in carrying signs and distributing leaflets. Company officials met with local Sheriff Leslie Goforth and Grant County district attorney Thomas Foy. The sheriff said he needed more deputies to intervene, so the company provided the funds to hire twenty special deputies. Empire Zinc officials then requested a restraining order from Grant County district judge Archibald Marshall to try impeding and ending the women's strike. The judge immediately issued the order. A general strike was contemplated by union members, but they decided not to go against the injunction. They all voted on having the women continue with the strike. The women succeeded in defending the picket lines.

On June 16, 1951, Sheriff Goforth along with his new force of deputies and hired strike breakers from out of state mounted a massive assault on the Hispanic women and children. They flung canisters of tear gas while shouting and yelling racist epithets. They also used wood batons while pushing the protestors around. The men used as much force available to them to try to disperse the crowd. Goforth and his men succeeded in arresting forty-five women and seventeen children. When this happened, many more women and children joined in on the strike. Officers dragged them on the ground crying and screaming. A child was run over by a car. Many required medical attention, but it was not provided. Officers threw the women and children in the backs of trucks and took them to Silver City, where they were booked and photographed. The women and their children faced a multitude of charges, including criminal trespassing, assault and injury of peace officers, vandalism and resisting arrest. District attorney Thomas Foy contacted New Mexico Governor Edwin Mechem for assistance by sending in the New Mexico State Police and the New Mexico Army National Guard. Foy was stunned when the governor failed to honor his request but instead ordered the immediate release of the women and children. The governor added in a statement that the New Mexico State Police could not legally serve as strike breakers. On June 24, 1951, the Federal Mediation and Conciliation Service called for arbitration of the issues. Empire Zinc officials once again refused to mediate.

The strikes in New Mexico were seen as communist subversion. When strike breakers and special Empire Zinc "deputies" charged at the women on August 23, 1951, and pulled them out of the strike lines, complete disorder ensued. The women gathered up rocks and swung them at the men. It is written the women also threw ground-up red chile powder at the men, some of whom apparently cried out as their eyes burned. The men pulled off the bandanas from the women and used these effectively as zip ties to bind the hands and feet of the women leaders. An undetermined number of women and their children were incarcerated in the county jail. Then demonstrations and sit-down protests took place at the sheriff's office and the Silver City newspaper offices. The newspaper claimed the men were physically injured and were impaired. In court, Judge Archibald Marshall asked Governor Mechem to declare martial law, the temporary rule of the region by military authorities. The governor instead ordered the state police to replace the "special deputies." The judge levied $4,000 fines on representatives of both the local and national unions and a ninety-day term in jail. New Mexico State Police Chief Joseph Roach and Captain John Bradford said they could keep the peace. However, the governor withdrew the state police when the stalemate continued. *Silver City Daily Press* editor Todd Ely wrote a blistery remark about the strikers, saying, "Mexico, of course, is poverty stricken because early settlers lost their identity in a mestizo melting pot that lowered the general level of culture to a point little above that of the swarming aborigines."

Empire Zinc got the full support of the district judge, sheriff, district attorney, Silver City magistrate judge and editor of the *Silver City Daily Press* newspaper. Most of the white residents also fully supported the company. The New Mexico protests and strike, which were making headlines nationally, resulted in a film being made with the title *Salt of the Earth*. "You are the salt of the earth, but if salt has lost its taste, how shall its saltiness be restored? It is no longer good for anything except to be thrown out and trampled under people's feet." (Matthew 5:13)

Academy Award–winning writer Michael Wilder contacted union miners in southern New Mexico about doing a film version of what was taking place with their strike and protests against Empire Zinc. The film script was written by Wilder, who went on-site and worked as he viewed the protests from a hill. *Salt of the Earth* was produced by Paul Jarrico and directed by Herbert J. Biberman under the auspices of the Liberty Film Company. Michael Wilder wrote or cowrote twenty-two screenplays. He was co-winner of an Academy Award for Best Adapted Screenplay for *A Place in the Sun* in 1951. He won an Edgar Award and another Oscar nomination for his script for *5 Fingers* in 1953. Wilson also worked on the script for the film *The Bridge on the River Kwai* in 1957, *5 Branded Women* produced by Laurence De Laurentis in 1960 and the script for *Lawrence of Arabia* in 1963. He also wrote the screenplay for *Planet of the Apes* in 1968 and the film *Che!* in 1969, which follows the life of Ernesto "Che" Guevara when he first landed in Cuba from Argentina in 1956 until his death in 1969. Guevara was a charismatic revolutionary figure who fascinated his followers. Guevara became one of the great heroes of the counterculture of the 1960s, and posters of his image served as an inspiration for the Chicano movement in the United States. Che Guevara made a famous visit to the United Nations in 1964. Omar Sharif played the lead role in this film.

Paul Jarrico was the producer of *Salt of the Earth*. He had a stellar career with Metro Goldwyn Mayer pictures. His 1941 film *Tom, Dick, and Harry*, starring Ginger Rogers, was nominated for an Academy Award for Best Original Screenplay. Director Herbert J. Biberman was a member of the Directors Guild of America. He was the cowriter and director of the film *Slaves*, produced in 1969. The lead actors were Ozzie Davis and Dionne Warwick. The film, set in the South in the 1850s, was about slaves sold to a sadistic plantation owner. In this film, Davis fights for his freedom against a cruel overseer. The other slaves join him in a revolt. This groundbreaking film, which showed the plight of slaves and the horror of slavery, was entered into the Cannes Film Festival in 1969. It was seen by mostly Black moviegoers in the United States and attacked by film critics and reviewers.

The musical score of *Salt of the Earth* was done by Sol Kaplan. He performed as a concert pianist before he turned to composing musical scores for film and television. During World War II, Kaplan composed music for the film units of the United States Army and the Office of Strategic Services, the precursor of the Central Intelligence Agency (CIA). He wrote the scores for thirty films, including *The Spy Who Came in from the Cold*, starring Richard Burton. Kaplan's score for *Tales of Manhattan* was nominated for an Academy Award.

The making of *Salt of the Earth* in New Mexico was highly original in scope and an innovative development. Most of the actors were the miners who had gone on strike, their wives and children. The locations were filmed in the actual sites of the strike. The writer, producer and director wanted as much authenticity as possible to capture the essence of the event that captured the public. A lead actor, Juan Chacón, was a mining leader and native New Mexican with no acting experience. Chacon was born in Dwyer, New Mexico, in November 1919 and died in Deming, New Mexico, on February 16, 1985. He served as president of Local 890 of the Amalgamated United Steelworkers Union for seventeen years. He recalled, "One guy had a gun in my chest" while being filmed in *Salt of the Earth*. He was not only steadfast but also supported by the other miners. After the film was produced, *Time* magazine said in review, "The best of the worker-players is Juan Chacon, real life president of the local union. Ugly and cold as an Aztec amulet, his heavy face comes slowly to life and warmth as the picture advances and in the end seems almost radiant."

Established Mexican film actress Rosaura Revueltas Sánchez was the only professional actress on set in Silver City. She came from an accomplished family that included a composer, a writer and a painter. Revueltas Sánchez was a screen and stage actor, dancer, teacher and author. She studied acting and ballet in Mexico City. She said she based her career on the better representation of women not only on film but in all careers. She immigrated to the United States via New Mexico and became proficient in English.

Right from the start, the film about the miners' strike against Empire Zinc was tainted by controversy, threats and verbal and physical assaults. It was claimed the miners' union in New Mexico had a subversive nature by those who did not want the film made and who did everything they could to sabotage the production. United States Congressman Donald L. Jackson from California told Congress the film was a "diabolical attack upon the United States" and a "new weapon for Russia" that would "depict the United States as the enemy of all colored peoples." Before the script was written and the film was developed, Michael Wilder, Herbert J. Biberman, Paul Jarrico and Sol Kaplan were subpoenaed to appear before the House Un-American Activities Committee (HUAC) to answer questions. They had been accused of being Communists. The period during which this committee was in action was called the Red Scare and Red Hunt. Another word used interchangeably for alleged disloyalty to the country was called "McCarthyism" after United States Senator Joseph McCarthy.

The HUAC under the House of Congress in Washington, D.C., was established in 1938. The sole purpose was to investigate American citizens, public employees and any organization suspected of fostering Communist ties. There was a frenzy of perceived rebellious activities against the country. Anyone accused was considered guilty without proof or evidence. There was a very thin line between the separation of civil liberties in contrast to the interests of national security.

In 1947, purported Communist influence on the motion picture industry in Hollywood took center stage. The focus of the HUAC was labor unions, labor union members, university and college professors, radio commentators, actors and screenwriters. Once the accused was taken to respond to questions before Congress, the mere fact of their appearance was slanted. They were considered guilty by association. If anyone refused to answer the pointed questioning, they were held in contempt of Congress and served a term of one year or more imprisonment. Leading Hollywood actors including Humphrey Bogart and Katharine Hepburn were called to defend themselves before the committee. In the end, over three hundred film directors, radio commentators, actors and screenwriters were boycotted in Hollywood. Absolutely no one was allowed to deal with them in any way or else they would also be subject to questioning. A mere 10 percent of those ostracized were able to regain their careers in the film industry.

Meanwhile, back in New Mexico, Biberman, who had been accused of being a Nazi spy although he was Jewish, was collaborating with Jarrico and Kaplan to produce *Salt of the Earth*. They genuinely thought it would be their last hurrah, especially since they had been blacklisted by the powerful and infamous HUAC in Washington, D.C. They were placed permanently on the Blacklist, those who were determined guilty and were avoided and spied on. According to an article that appeared in the September 1954 issue of *La Crónica* (*The Chronicle*), the Hollywood Film Council and the Motion Picture Industry Council along with the Screen Actors Guild all asked for a federal investigation of the subversive nature of the union and the impending film. This meant much difficulty in finding camera men, actors, a film crew, production managers—all those necessary to produce a movie. The determined men finally went with having the actual miners and their families play most of the roles. On March 8, 1953, the main union meeting halls in the nearby cities of Carlsbad and Bayard were both deliberately burned down. The home of lead actress Rosaura Revueltas was raided, and all her possessions were confiscated. She was deported. Cameramen were beaten, and their cameras were damaged or destroyed. Production manager Jules Sherwin stated they were all threatened with bullets and black boxes, a reference to being killed and leaving in coffins. The chief editor of the film was paid off by the FBI to quit and prevent the film from being released.

The idealized version of American society totally ignored the social unrest sweeping across the country. Minorities were unseen on the screen and television except in negative portrayals. The cavalry and wagon train masters along with pioneers defeated Indians who terrorized poor settlers and innocent travelers. Mexican servants named María and José graciously served considerate American whites. The *bandidos* in black sombreros felt the wrath of courageous lawmen and heroes in white hats. No self-respecting family was involved in the battles of racial segregation, the Vietnam War or marches for women's rights. The women of Salt of the Earth were in total contrast to acceptable conventional forms. They bathed in and washed clothes in galvanized metal tubs. They chopped wood for cooking stoves and to boil water to wash dishes. They struggled along with their husbands to feed the family, which often included extended members such as the elderly. The women tied their hair in buns and most often wore bandanas, large patterned or colored handkerchiefs on the head. These were worn in church, outside of home or while working. A few women wore pants. This was seen as an outrage. Quite often grandfathers, husbands, uncles and cousins worked at the mines as well as close friends. Therefore, the women were also related or were bosom friends. It was not altogether surprising that the women chose to stand in for their husbands to continue the strike against Empire Zinc. When their spouses were threatened with incarceration, the women stood firm, unyielding and determined. Many were thrown in jail along with their kids. From behind the prison bars, they cried out for justice. Their strong voices, along with their prayers, could not be silenced.

A line pronounced by actress Rosaura Revueltas Sánchez in the movie went straight to the point: "Our roots go deep in this place, deeper than the pines, deeper than the mine shaft." She was arrested for an alleged Mexican passport violation and was forcibly detained by U.S. immigration officials along with the FBI. She exclaimed, "They had no evidence to present my subversive character! I can only conclude that I was dangerous because I had been playing a role that gave status and dignity to the character of a Mexican American woman."

United States Congressman Donald Jackson proclaimed, "A Communist movie being filmed at Silver City, New Mexico, is deliberately designed to inflame racial hatred and harm the United States in the eyes of the world.... It emphasizes alleged mistreatment of Mexicans in the country."

The film was forced to be made outside of the Hollywood studio system. News reporters were barred from the filming area by Empire Zinc. Filming sets were relocated to a remote area near Bayard, New Mexico. Hispanics in Silver City movie theaters were separated from the Anglos. They also could not go into certain restaurants. The strike complicated matters. Music was blared from speakers to disrupt the filming. The cast and crew were assaulted, and the home of one of the actors was burned down. Continued harassment during and since the outset of the strike included strikebreakers hired by the company who were referred to as "scabs." These were miners who had rejected joining the labor union. Thus, they were free to continue working under the conditions that created the problem in the first place. Some who had infiltrated meetings held by union members updated Zinc Empire officials as to what the union was planning. Some of these informants were on the company's payroll. They were involved in name calling and used slur tactics on the strikers. Juan Chacon stated, "They asked me if my wife or I wore the pants in my family. I couldn't answer."

Since the movie could not be shown in the United States and everyone associated with it was ostracized, it was picked up in China, Europe and other countries. Under the Chinese Communist regime of Mao Tse Tung, the New Mexico film was shown many times. They wanted to see why this movie caused such a hullabaloo in the United Sates. In East Germany, *Salt of the Earth* was shown as a human rights film. In Paris, *Salt of the Earth* was shown at a function equivalent to the Academy Awards, called the Academie du Cinema de Paris in 1955. It won Best Foreign Film of the Year. New Mexico native Juan Chacon received critical acclaim as Best Actor, surpassing established actors with some from Hollywood in movies dubbed in French. Although *Salt of the Earth* was an assault on free expression, it became a popular cult film. It was deemed "culturally significant" by the United States Library of Congress and one of the one hundred most noteworthy films ever produced in Hollywood out of thousands. It is preserved in the National Film Registry for posterity as an enduring cinematic classic not only worthy of preservation but of strong significance of prejudice and racial profiling in the United States.

The Empire Zinc Company closed permanently in New Mexico in 1969. The company never restored its reputation after its confrontation with the indomitable spirit of New Mexico's miner's wives, grandmothers and daughters. The valorous ladies would not give up and faced up to the odds that were stacked against them. It was their upbringing. It was their history. In May 2022, a commemoration was held and a bronze plaque was installed at the site of the women's persevering strike that gained national and international attention. During the well-attended ceremony, several descendants and original participants spoke. One recalled that her mother was fifteen years old and her aunt was eighteen when they were both thrown in jail along with the others. Gilbert Cruz Diaz proclaimed, "The sheriff hit my father's mother-in-law and broke her arm." For well over a year, over one hundred women, many with children, dauntlessly stood their ground. Rachel Valencia recalled:

> *I was only fourteen, when a fast-moving deputy's car sped by me, I grabbed onto the hood so I wouldn't get run over. I held on for my life as it sped up. I finally let go and rolled on the dirt. I got up coughing and choking. The beautiful dress my mother had sewed was ripped and torn. My hair was full of dirt. I saw Consuelo Martínez, an old woman was killed by the same car, when I looked over. There was blood everywhere. Her family had to bury the poor old woman. What was happening to us was so terrible and sad. When other women came to help me, they put handcuffs on me. Those horrible men treated us very rough. They arrested all of us and took us to jail.*

The protestors all ranged in ages from infants in mothers' arms to ninety years old. The valorous women said, "Great affliction and hardship made us stronger." This was the legacy these New Mexico women left for those who would come after them.

Chapter 3

TORCHES PASSED ON

Among the prevalent voices during the period of social unrest in the 1960s, heard but seldom written about were those of the women. Dolores Huerta has been in the news continuously because of her connection to Cesar Chávez and the United Farmworkers Union in California. Huerta was born in New Mexico, also to farm laborers, and her family left immediately for California after her birth. She became very active in the struggle for the rights and just compensation of Mexican farmworkers. A name seldom heard but also quite relevant to this time and place in New Mexico is Josefina Adelaida Anaya.

Josefina Adelaida was born in Belen, Valencia County, New Mexico, on March 19, 1941. She was the daughter of Irenidad and Margaret Anaya. Her father owned a business in Belen. Sometime after graduating from Belen High School, Josefina became a legal assistant at the law firm attorney Dave Cargo was associated with in Albuquerque in 1960. When her husband, who was a Republican, decided to run for governor, Josefina campaigned heavily for him in the Democratic stronghold of northern New Mexico. She spoke Spanish fluently. In fact, during this period, New Mexico had for the most part leaned toward the Democratic Party, and few Republicans gained office. It was an obstacle Cargo hoped he could overcome. He had already served in the New Mexico legislature as a state representative. After marriage, Josefina Adelaida was better known as Ida Jo Cargo.

Ida Jo had the ingrained ability to attract well-known community leaders to her husband's political aspirations. Cargo's young wife, who was

Social justice activist Dolores Huerta is shown leading a protest march in the south valley of Albuquerque. *Courtesy of and by Arnold Trujillo.*

only twenty-four at the time, helped bolster his crossover appeal to older and younger Hispanic voters across New Mexico. Ida Jo and her husband campaigned in the back of an old pickup truck. The young woman was described as feisty and extremely independent. People referred to Ida Jo as New Mexico's Jackie Kennedy because of her stylish dress, which mimicked the popular first lady and wife of President Kennedy. Belen resident José Campos said Josefina Adelaida was called the "wild-eyed revolutionary from Belen." Ida Jo became known as La Politiquera, the Political One. Ida Jo was well known for her background in New Mexico's civil rights movement. She became a leading spirit in public affairs, and this drew many people in.

One such person was my own father, Maximo "Max" de Aragón. He was a traveling salesman who had connections throughout New Mexico. My dad would say at home, "I wore out several pairs of shoes campaigning for Cargo." Although my father was a staunch Democrat, he strongly supported Cargo's plans to help the poor of the northern part of the state, especially the county of Mora, where my mother and her extensive family came from. Each morning for several weeks, Maximo would pick up campaign material at Cargo's headquarters in Albuquerque. When he would travel to places such as Belen, Santa Fe, Pecos, Las Vegas and many outlying towns and villages, he would take along plenty of campaign material.

Ray John de Aragón presenting at the Ninth Annual National Latino Writers Conference held at the National Hispanic Cultural Center in Albuquerque in May 2011. Nationally and internationally recognized Latino writers were invited, including de Aragón, who was honored at the event. *Author's collection.*

Lonesome Dave Cargo was twice elected governor of New Mexico and served from 1967 to 1971. As the twenty-second governor, he remains one of the youngest governors ever elected in United States history. At the age of twenty-five, Ida Jo Cargo was the youngest first lady in New Mexico history. It was publicized by the media that the first lady was a candid member of Reies López Tijerina's Alianza movement. Understandably, Ida Jo lost favor around some political figures and wealthy patrons of the governor. She was a descendant of the Belen Land Grant and the extensive Nicolas Duran y Chávez Land Grant. This Spanish grant was stolen by a group of land speculators who moved into the area. Several events took place during Cargo's administration that made national news.

Antiwar demonstrations at many college campuses were occurring across the United States. In a journal archive on February 12, 1966, there was an article that stated:

> *Silent demonstrators shivered in the cold and suffered insults but no physical injuries Friday at the University of New Mexico as they started a planned 24-hour "vigil" to protest U.S. Viet Nam policies. The silent vigil, around a "coffin" labeled "Here lies the dignity of the U.S. of A."…The number of silent protesters, in "mourning" around the coffin, ranged from a couple to 15 throughout most the day. They did not carry signs although members carried leaflets which cited Abraham Lincoln's opposition to the Mexican War.…We now protest a war which is infinitely more degrading and shameful to the U.S.*

New Mexico National Guard troops were sent to the UNM campus to quell any planned marches and protests. The Guardsmen were to use teargas and dummy rubber bullets. It is estimated there were close to seven hundred students involved, including students from the University of Albuquerque, New Mexico Highlands University and other New Mexico college campuses.

New Mexico Army Guardsmen bayoneted several students. Naturally, chaos erupted. Many students were injured. Over one hundred students were arrested and jailed.

Dave Cargo served as New Mexico governor during the turbulent period from 1967 to 1971. His marriage to Ida Jo Cargo ended in divorce. Lonesome Dave moved to another state; he later returned to New Mexico and ran for several other high offices but failed. The events at Tierra Amarilla and at the University of New Mexico were still on people's minds.

Ida Jo Cargo and other women left their mark on New Mexico history. There were several others directly involved with the movement for social justice in the state. Elizabeth "Betita" Martínez was very active as a young award-winning reporter of the civil rights movement. She worked as a reporter for a newspaper called *El Grito del Norte* (*Cry of the North*). Other writers such as Clarissa Rojas praised Martínez for her involvement and struggles in bringing out vital issues of social justice movements to the public. Martínez wrote *Elizabeth: A Chicana Icon Who Brought Joy to Protest.* Martínez was the editor of *500 Años del Pueblo Chicano* (*500 Years of Chicano History in Pictures*), published by SWOP, the Southwest Organizing Project, in Albuquerque, New Mexico, in 1992.

A march for social justice and civil rights in Las Vegas New Mexico, led by *El Grito del Norte* newspaper icon Elizabeth "Betita" Martínez. *Photo by Adelita Medina.*

Members of the La Raza Unida political party and Chicanos para-Justicia converge at the Old Town Park in Las Vegas, New Mexico, in 1972 to stage a protest against injustice. Juan José Peña, *kneeling at far right*, became a faculty instructor of Chicano Studies at New Mexico Highlands University. *Photo by Adelita Medina.*

Elizabeth Martínez, along with Enriqueta Vásquez, Adelita Medina and others, provided a road in print and pictures for others to read and see, thereby creating not only a vision but also a lasting image of a movement affecting everyone in America. *El Grito del Norte* was a bilingual newspaper located in Española. It was originally published by Reies López Tijerina and his Alianza. In Española, the popular periodical was co-founded by Martínez and Beverly Axelrod in 1968.

Along this vein, *La Escuela Padre Don Antonio José Martínez* was established in Montezuma, New Mexico, near the city of Las Vegas. In March 1973, Archbishop James Peter Davis of the Archdiocese of Santa Fe publicly announced that the community organizations known as Montezuma Unidos, in reference to a group of the residents of Montezuma, and Chicano Unidos Para Justicia (Chicanos United for Justice), advancing veteran health services and educational programs, would be granted use of buildings at the former Montezuma seminary. The location was the famous Montezuma Hotel with extensive buildings and grounds. The plans of the two citizen groups from nearby towns was the establishment of an alternative school that would incorporate a curriculum that included social justice issues and history. When the school served students from northern

New Mexico, it was named Escuela Antonio José Martínez, after new Mexico's folk hero priest. Adelita Michelle Medina served as the academic coordinator at the school. She recalls:

> *The school was named after revered northern New Mexico priest, Padre Antonio José Martínez, who was a champion of the poor, creating educational opportunities for Hispanics, Indians, and girls. As a priest he took very progressive stands on many issues; for example, he refused to collect tithes from the poor and he opposed large grants of land to individuals, saying the land should go to the people.*

Adelita Medina was a founder of Chicanos Unidos Para Justicia, a grassroots organization dedicated to fighting against injustice and racism and for the self-determination of Chicano communities that supported the basis for La Escuela. At the school, she taught older students the basics of photography and how to process the film in the dark room. She also founded and edited a newspaper called *Tierra y Libertad* (*Land and Liberty*). Medina worked with the social justice newspaper *El Grito del Norte* from 1971 to 1973. She wrote numerous articles, took many photos and worked on the layout for the popular paper. As a recognized journalist, she went to Wounded Knee to photograph protests and report on the takeover there by the American Indian Movement (AIM), an American Indian grassroots movement that was spearheaded and influenced by other civil rights organizations. AIM was founded in Minnesota in 1968. This social justice group addressed systemic and historical underlying problems of racial discrimination in the country against Native Americans. It also brought attention to the poverty experienced by Indians. AIM was the driving force of the Indian civil rights movement sweeping the nation and the long history of a multitude of broken treaties by the U.S. government that led to the takeover of uncounted millions of acres of choice lands.

In 1953, with the "Termination Policy," the United States Congress officially ended recognition of over one hundred tribes. Native Americans were prompted to move out of reservations and into cities with the intent of assimilating them into the social mix, another method of incorporating additional Indian lands into what had already been taken in years past. In the cities, Native Americans encountered not only extreme racism, poverty, alcohol and drugs but also homelessness and profiling by police. They also had no access to health or educational benefits. Starting on February 27, 1973, AIM took over the Wounded Knee, South Dakota site of a horrendous

Campesinas, acrylic on canvas painting, by Adelita Medina, 2019, features women farmworkers in the fields. The artist says, "Women were essential workers who also struggled to put food on the table." *Courtesy Adelita Medina.*

massacre of Indians in 1890 by United States cavalry troops. Adelita M. Medina was permitted to photograph and report on the massive protests that took place there, which lasted nearly three months.

In the 1980s, Medina worked for the Center of Constitutional Rights in New York City. She was coordinator of the Movement Support Network

Young schoolchildren at the Escuela Antonio José Martínez in Montezuma, New Mexico, display solidarity in seeking social justice for all Hispanic children and youth. *Photo by Adelita Medina.*

(MSN), which was a national project that lent support to organizations doing work on Central American issues. The work done by MSN resulted in the convening of congressional hearings to investigate the cases it had documented and question the involvement of the FBI and other government agencies in suppressing the rights of activist organizations and individuals. Medina went on to focus on her artwork, which in many cases depicts the plight of people. She curated her first arts event, called *WE the People/El Pueblo Unido for Peace, Justice, and Mother Earth*. She currently works as a fund consultant for *Alianza* Nacional de Campesinos, Inc., a California-based organization created by and for women farmworkers. She holds a master of science degree from Columbia University Graduate School of Journalism.

The Land of Enchantment in New Mexico provided the perfect backdrop for hippie exploration of the people and the land. Much of the land was composed of an agrarian society among the Hispanic and Native American populations. Hippies at first were an oddity in the larger cities such as Albuquerque. Hispanic *parteras*, or midwives, were sought out to deliver babies. *Curanderas* (Hispanic medicine women) taught the use of medicinal herbs and roots to anyone willing to learn about the benefits of certain plants to cure illnesses. Large hippie communes were established

Jesús "Chuy" Martínez annually coordinates a major event honoring Dolores Huerta with programs taking place at the National Hispanic Cultural Center and the Albuquerque Southwest valley. *Courtesy Arnold Trujillo.*

in certain areas, such as Ocate and even on the grounds of Montezuma, where they bathed in the natural medicinal hot springs located there. Some complaints emerged when communes were set up on Hispanic private lands or areas where residents were not very happy with the turn of events. Then on June 20, 1971, New Mexico's hippie movement made national news. A headline in the *New York Times* read, "Albuquerque Divided Over Cause of First Major Riot."

Reporter Martin Waldron wrote that on Sunday, June 19, hundreds of hippies and youth from the Mexican American community, as he called it, gathered at Roosevelt Park for a major music festival featuring local and out-of-state bands. Albuquerque city police were notified to check up on things, so they arrived in several squad cars and in riot gear. They saw some in the crowd drinking beer and smoking marijuana, so officers immediately arrested some of the males and females. This sparked up the rest of the large crowd when individuals were frisked and searched. It was not written how many were arrested, but forty-one were injured, with fifteen by gunfire, and Waldron wrote that fire-bombs destroyed automobiles and resulted in broken window storefronts. The vandalism and damage stretched along several miles of Route 66 (now called Central Avenue). Calm was restored in the city when the New Mexico Army National Guard and the Air Guard from nearby Kirtland Air Force Base were called up. City Commission Chairman Harry E. Kinney and other city officials wondered why all of this happened. Waldron wrote:

> *The Black Berets, a "brown power" movement with some Negro membership, said they had been shouting into a vacuum of warnings about unemployment, frustration and what they see as racism and police brutality.…In 1967, the state had its first case of brown-power violence. Reies Tijerina, a Fundamentalist protestant preacher from Texas, led an uprising of the desperately poor in northern New Mexico. Tijerina's men seized a whole county, contending that the land was theirs because it had been stolen from trusting Mexican, Spanish and Indian settlers by immigrating Anglos. Tijerina wound up in prison…but the fire he started in 1967 has never gone out.*

All the arts, including visual, literary and performing, took up the rise in social activism. This contributed immensely to the civil rights movement not only in the United States but internationally. Theater plays a critical role in shaping the meaning of realism through telling history with words and drama. Theater places things into context by taking events and people into words and actions and how they happened. This is an exploration, a quest for discovery that takes dynamic actions and makes them vibrant and living with dialogue and emotion. It is an orchestration of costuming in conjunction with movement and color, thrusting the action taking place on stage out onto the audience. It makes for a more engaging and transformative experience.

Playwright and artistic director of New Mexico Matraka, Inc. Rosa María Calles stated:

The announcement of a celebration honoring Chicano activist Juan José Peña on June 7, 2023. *Courtesy Ralph Arellanes.*

> *I wanted to generate a discussion among viewers and have them reflect on our true history, not the one fabricated by historians from other cultures who wrote about our people and explained who we are and why we do what we do. This would be an empowering tool that embraces all the arts by using imagination and remodeling our society through the telling of our stories. My story of La Llorona was one of gender inequality and about being judged by society depending on one's wealth or status symbol. I wanted to challenge stereotypes, and social justice issues that resonate with current issues and problems. The real story of Padre Martínez is one of resilience and survival. It is a compelling story crafted to harness the power of theater not simply for entertainment but to inspire change.*

Albuquerque City Mayor Tim Keller holding a bronze plaque on June 9, 2023, during the dedication ceremony of the civil rights activist Don Juan José Peña Plaza at Barelas Park. *Photo by Ralph Arellanes.*

Luis Valdez, founder and artistic director of El Teatro Campesino in California, sought to dramatize the distressing conditions of farmworkers. Migrant farmworkers circulated throughout the fields not only in California but also in Texas, Arizona and New Mexico. They performed backbreaking labor picking chile in the vast fields of New Mexico, along with fruit and vegetables. In California, grape pickers were not only discriminated against but also lived in poverty and horrendous working conditions. This was the cause of Luis Valdez, who began with simple plays that grew into a powerful force that drew national attention. His production *Zoot Suit*, based partially on the Zoot Suit Riots that took place in Los Angeles in 1942, was Valdez's most successful drama. Military personnel stripped the suits off Mexican American youth, as they objected to their style of clothing and look. Zoot suiters in Albuquerque around the same period were also discriminated against in newspapers and on radio. The young Hispanic men and women were targeted on the street by police and at dances. When *Zoot Suit* was performed at the National Hispanic Cultural Center in Albuquerque, it drew a great deal of attention from the public because some of the actual Zoot Suiters from New Mexico or their families attended the performances. Zoot Suit culture in New Mexico was comparable to that in California. Teatro Campesino (Rural Theater) is indicative of country life. Other terms used are rustic or simple, but there is nothing simple that begins with a soft rain and then these whispering drops of water can grow into a torrent.

These were also the thoughts of José Rodríguez when he sought to create La Companía de Teatro de Alburquerque with the help of Dr. Miguel Encinias, director of the Multicultural Center at the University of Albuquerque. Later as a priest, Rodríguez was inspired by the life and times of Padre Martínez of Taos. He had taken up the torch passed on by the legacy of the folk hero priest of New Mexico. Rodríguez first said when arriving in New Mexico and seeing the Sandia Mountains adjacent to Albuquerque, "I had never

Tres Vatos, acrylic painting by upcoming artist Rosalinda Pacheco, vividly portrays Chicano youth during the civil rights movement that sought social justice. *Courtesy Rosalinda Pacheco.*

Announcement of a performance of *La Pasión de Jesús Chávez* (*The Passion of Jesús Chávez*) at Ilfeld Auditorium in Las Vegas, New Mexico, on April 16 and 17, 1988. The sold-out performances were featured in *Visions of New Mexico Magazine* and theater journals. *Author's collection.*

seen mountains that were so big. There was infinite space around them. On my seeing them, I felt the whole area was a natural spirit from God. I felt something very special about all of it. I could feel it was given to me, and that this would be my next home."

José Rodríguez was born in San Juan, Puerto Rico. He had been interested in drama since he was a young boy, and he sought every opportunity to do any performance in grade school and high school. In time, Rodríguez graduated from the Royal Academy of the Dramatic Arts in London, England. He then became a member of the Spanish Repertory Company of New York. The Repertory Theater group performed in Albuquerque, and it was then that José Rodríguez, as a lead performer in a play, was exposed to New Mexico and became determined to make the state his home. His opportunity came when Dr. Miguel Encinias formed La Companía de Teatro de Albuquerque. Encinias had been so impressed with Rodríguez when he saw the young actor perform that he offered him the job of artistic director of the new theatrical company. Rodríguez immediately took up the new position, and accolades started pouring in for his work. He was offered the lead role of a movie based on Oscar Romero, a martyred priest from Latin America. He declined the role because he had just been ordained a priest and he had to make a choice—actor or priest? Actor Raul Julia then took the role of Bishop Oscar Arnulfo Romero, and the film appeared on-screen in 1989. It received the Christopher Award in 1989. In 1991, it was a Political Film, USA Human Rights nominee. The film was also an Academy Award nominee. Rothko Chapel established the Oscar Romero Award for the recognition of individuals and organizations exercising courageous, grassroots human rights advocacy to further civil rights in the United States.

Bishop Romero served as a prelate in the Latin American country of El Salvador. He was an outspoken critic against the violent activities of the government. Bishop Romero at the pulpit and in public became a heroic advocate of human rights. His deeds and activities caught the attention of the Vatican and the world. He was nominated for the Nobel Peace Prize in 1979. Oscar Romero constantly emphasized the continuous struggle of the poor for justice. Because of this, the popular bishop became a hated target of the government. He was assassinated while saying mass by a right-wing death squad. Pope Francis declared Bishop Oscar Romero a martyr of the Catholic Church, and he was canonized as a saint in March 2018.

The goal of La Companía was to present works by New Mexican writers on stage. Another focus was to stage a selection of classical works written by Latin American and Spanish writers. The theater company was an immediate success. La Companía was invited to perform at the fourth Siglo de Oro Chamizal International Drama Festival in 1979. Later, La Companía de Alburquerque was invited to perform at the Edinburgh Theater Festival in Scotland and at the Fourth Latin American Popular Theatre Festival in New York City in 1984. José Rodríguez wrote and produced *Nuevo Mexico, Si!*, a wildly popular drama featuring multiple vignettes of New Mexico history. One episode in the play was a dialogue between former Archbishop Jean Baptiste Lamy and Padre Don Antonio José Martínez drawn from the book *Padre Martínez and Bishop Lamy*. In the piece by Rodríguez, Bishop Lamy apologizes for his unacceptance of the priest and cultures of New Mexico, saying he was in a strange place and land and was overwhelmed by what he encountered as a young man that was totally different from his homeland in France. The production traveled widely, including several New Mexico cities.

However, Rodríguez considered his all-Spanish production *La Pasión de Jesús Chávez* (*The Passion of Jesús Chávez*), written and directed by him, as his best work. He often recalled traveling in Mexico and a particular village he and a group went to. He said he was enjoying the scenery and the friendliness of the people and then went off on his own to see more. That is when a little boy and girl caught his attention. The girl was older than the boy and held a green banana in her hand. She then opened it up, and Rodríguez said she gave the banana to the boy and ate the peel:

> *I then saw things in a very different way. Instead of enjoying the landscape, I began to see the poverty that was around me. When I returned to New Mexico, I saw it there too. I opened my eyes, and my mind was open also. I began to write* La Pasión de Jesús Chávez. *I wanted to portray on stage, those that were rich and powerful in contrast to the needy and the helpless. I also tried to point out that the best way to attain peace and justice, was through nonviolence, and harmony.*

The masterful playwright showed that the means to this end resulted in the death of the village hero. The back-and-forth battle and resistance and the ensuing tragic clash were described beautifully by a ballad, composed and performed by the very talented and skilled Jesús "Chuy" Martínez, which he wrote for the play.

Right: The author in the lead dramatic role of Jesús Chávez at the eight-hundred-seat Ilfeld Auditorium in Las Vegas, New Mexico, in 1988. Chávez was a fictional social justice character in the play written, directed and produced by José Rodríguez, artistic director of La Compania de Teatro de Alburquerque. *Author's collection.*

Below: The author as social justice leader José Chávez lies on the theater floor after he is executed by a firing squad. The fictional Chávez captures the ire and anger of the government of a country in Latin America after he leads a popular revolt that spreads throughout the nation. *Author's collection.*

"El Corrido de Jesús Chávez"	**"The Ballad of Jesus Chavez"**
En el pueblo de Madera Del estado de Chihuahua Paso un caso interesante Que agarro toda la fama. Un hombre que sin sotana su amor a Dios entrego.	In the town of Madera In the state of Chihuahua An interesting case occurred which took all the fame. A man without a cassock gave his love to God.
Jesús Chávez se llamaba El campesino valiente. El que su vida a la gente A ayudarle dedico.	Jesús Chávez was the name of that valiant countryman giving his life to the people dedicated to helping them.
Tantos lugares se acuerdan De problemas resorbidos. Huellas que Jesús dejaba Por toditos los caminos. Lo recordaba la gente, Lo recordaban los niños.	Many places remember of problems resolved. Tracks Jesus left Through all the roads. People recalled, children remembered.
Jesús Chávez regreso Decía toda la gente, El campesino valiente Que los ricos humillo.	Jesús Chávez returned everyone said. The valiant countryman humiliated the rich.
La historia se repetía Del otro Jesús Divino, Aquel que a este mundo vino A pasar puros tormentos. Y el que dejo mandamientos que Jesús Chávez cumplió.	The history was repeated of the other Divine Jesus, the one who came to this world to face many torments. And he left commandments Jesús Chávez fulfilled.

Ernest Antonio Mares once recalled the book *Padre Martinez and Bishop Lamy* as a great pioneering work on the life of the famous priest of Taos. Tony Mares, as he was popularly known, was a recognized New Mexico poet who penned the well-known book of his work called *With the Eyes of a Raptor*. This monumental figure in New Mexico's poetry scene also wrote a widely

Famed New Mexico photographer Arnold Trujillo captured social justice activist Jesús "Chuy" Martínez in a photo that portrays the singer before audiences with his heartrending songs of protest and action. *Courtesy Arnold Trujillo.*

praised play based on his early life experiences titled *Lola's Last Dance*. The play was directed by Paola Martini and staged by Siembra, Latino Theater Season, along with Teatro Paraguas. However, Tony's main pride and work was his Chautauqua one-man characterization of Padre Martínez, which he performed for many years in a multitude of venues.

Mares wrote in *Padre Martínez: New Perspectives from Taos*, published by the Millicent Rogers Museum in 1988, "This book, one hopes, will inspire other historians, literary critics, and writers to explore and reveal new dimensions of the ever-fascinating figure of Padre Antonio José Martínez of Taos." Six essays—written by Ray John de Aragón, Thomas J. Steele, Patricia Clark Smith, Bette S. Weidman and E.A. Mares—present this famous historical figure of New Mexico from a variety of perspectives, such as social, political, religious and cultural. Along with the release of the book, the museum hosted an exhibit of artifacts related to Padre Martínez and presentations by the writers to a large audience of several hundred attendees at the Harwood Museum, also in Taos. The *Taos News* published a special insert of several pages that detailed the life and times of Padre Martínez for the New Mexico public. The priest was featured for his philanthropy in advancing human well-being in education, the arts, the government and the church through his charitable gifts of his time and money.

In 1992, the Hispanic Women's Council and the New Mexico Quincentenary Commission, along with the Center for Regional Studies at the University of New Mexico in conjunction with El Norte Publication/Academia, produced *Nuestras Mujeres*. This book featured New Mexican Hispanic women with images from 1582 until 1992. The book was edited by Tey Diana Rebolledo. This was followed by *Mujeres Valerosas* in 2006, a book produced by the Hispanic Women's Council. *Nuestras Mujeres* (*Our Women*) and *Mujeres Valerosas* (*Valorous Women*) feature extraordinary women who have impacted the lives of others. Aurora Lucero-White Lea lobbied for women's vote. Mari-Luci Jaramillo served as deputy assistant secretary for Latin American affairs and was U.S. ambassador to Honduras. Millie Santillanes founded the Hispanic Culture Preservation League and served as director of cultural services for the City of Albuquerque. All the women have challenged stereotypes, including New Mexico native and author Dr. Irene Blea, who received her PhD from the University of Colorado–Boulder and is well known and recognized in civil rights circles. She continues to be a public speaker and recalls what her situation was like as a young woman:

> *I was schooled in justice. I was taught very early that you know the power of your strength by the power of your enemy. My father was a steelworker and AFL-CIO union member. The American Federation of Labor and Congress of Industrial Organization strove to improve the lives of working people, and he frequently talked to me about human rights. Thus, I was ready for the Chicano movement and strongly disappointed about the sexism I encountered within it. I've devoted my life to address various elements of discrimination against women since that time by speaking, writing, and teaching about it as a university professor and now an online presence.*

Dr. Blea published two textbooks that are used in university classes. She is the author of *Toward a Chicano Social Science* and *La Chicana*. She retired from California State University–Los Angeles. She was a tenured full professor and the chairperson of the Mexican American Studies Department. Dr. Blea is included in *United States Chicanas and Latinas Within a Global Context* and in *La Chicana and the Intersection of Race, Class and Gender*, which explores the evolution of Hispanic women onto the national scene

Dr. Irene Blea, a nationally recognized proponent of issues affecting Chicana/Hispanic women, is pictured with the Reverend Jesse Jackson in Albuquerque. Jackson was supporting Dr. Blea's outrage at the proposed elimination of Chicano Studies classes at the University of New Mexico. *Courtesy Dr. Irene Blea.*

in politics, health, economics, education, religion and criminal justice and focuses on participation in social movements.

An integral part of any movement dedicated to social justice is protest art. Pablo Picasso's world-famous *La Guernica* readily comes to mind. The famous artist was protesting the bombing of the town of Guernica in Spain by Adolf Hitler's Luftwaffe, the Nazi Air Force. It was simply a test of the might of Germany's air force, authorized by General Francisco Franco, the leader of Spain. Innocent people died, buildings were destroyed and many suffered at the expense of a test. Picasso was outraged. He displayed his resentment and anger with his paints and brushes on a massive scale. During the period of racial tension and unrest in America in the 1960s and '70s, the arts of music, dance, theater and paint came into play. Murals graced walls to bring attention to the plight of people. Muralist Francisco LeFebre recalls those vibrant days and the meaning of mural arts today:

> *The importance of mural art is that people must have something with which they can identify themselves with. The expression of a people's culture is extremely important. I thought and think it is my duty to express what my people and the times are all about on walls. I do murals with the same confidence that a farmer laboriously tills the soil. He waits for the fruits of his labor to sprout. I wait for the toils of my work to burst out and make an impact. When I was young, I got caught up in the Chicano movement.*

New Mexico Highlands University in Las Vegas was the scene of protests and marches. I was fortunate to be given the opportunity to do a mural at the student Union Building. It was an area most people had to drive by so it would be seen daily by anyone going through this very busy route. I chose to feature Ernesto "Che" Guevara, the revolutionary leader of Cuba, that was being glorified as a hero throughout the Latin American world. At Highlands we did a total of ten murals from 1971 to 1972. They could have been called radical murals, but they were strictly cultural. The muralist expresses himself in a political and philosophical sense. I believed that the greater the political convictions, the greater one becomes as a true artista. *"Che" Guevara stood as a symbol of self-determination and struggle against oppression. He was also against racial discrimination, and class exploitation in revolutionary Cuba. He was popularized by the Chicano resistance culture of the period, so I believed this was an appropriate figure to portray, especially at Highlands University where students were involved in raising up opportunities for Hispanics as educational leaders at university campuses not only in New Mexico but around the country. "Che" Guevara's trademark was his wearing a black beret. This was adopted by the Black Panthers, and New Mexico's Black Berets. Both groups also emulated the rest of his style of dress.*

New Mexico native Francisco LeFebre studied mural art in Mexico City at the San Carlos Art Academy. He worked on murals in Mexico, Chile and Cuba. In New Mexico, he and Irene Oliver Lewis, Jesús "Chuy" Martínez and Bernadette Rodriguez founded El Centro Cultural de Nuevo Mexico, the Cultural Center of New Mexico, with its home in Albuquerque. Since LeFebre had been very actively involved with Chicano muralism in northern New Mexico, he spearheaded the painting of one in the South Valley of Albuquerque at the Barelas Community Center. It showed a horse clearing out the flames he portrayed as the challenges of survival. LeFebre helped with the Southwest Organizing Project to develop community youth murals in Albuquerque. The well-known muralist was involved as the head of the North Valley Community Center, which was opened to serve area Santeros

Opposite: Famed muralist and painter Francisco LeFebre was caught up in the Chicano movement for civil rights. He was given permission to paint a large mural of Cuba's Che Guevara, who became an idolized figure in the movement at New Mexico Highlands University during the height of national social justice activities in the 1960s. *Courtesy Francisco LeFebre.*

Above: A protest in front of New Mexico Highlands University administrative offices when Chicano Studies as a discipline was being removed. *Photo by and courtesy of Adelita Medina.*

(woodworkers sculpting wooden religious art). It was also a venue for theater groups such as Matraka, Inc., which held regular rehearsals at the center for large-scale theatrical productions such as *Cuento de La Llorona* and *Padre Martínez, the Grey Eminence of Taos*. LeFebre was also actively involved as a board member of NALAC (National Association of Latino Arts and Culture). He hosted a regional convention in Albuquerque with acclaimed authors Rudolfo Anaya and Ray John de Aragón. He also helped organize the international NALAC conventions that were held in San Antonio and Corpus Christi, Texas. Themes for his work continue to be drawn from the history and traditions of New Mexico, which still serve as the inspiration for his highly recognized and acclaimed work.

"*Tierra y Libertad*—Land and Liberty" was a battle cry heard often during the Alianza movement of the 1960s in New Mexico. These powerful words

County artist speaks at Latino art meet

BY SANDY BATTIN
NEWS-BULLETIN STAFF WRITER

Valencia County author Ray John de Aragon will be addressing the National Association of Latino Arts and Culture as a keynote speaker on "La Cultura Hispanica de Nuevo Mexico" this weekend.

De Aragon, who is most widely known for his book, "Hermanos de la Luz," on the history of the Penitentes, will speak at the conference on the history of santero art as part of the tale of New Mexico.

"I won't be touching just folk art but the fine arts," he said. "And I'll be talking about the problems Hispanic artists found in being recognized and shown in galleries."

Although de Aragon was raised in Las Vegas, N.M., his wife Rosa María Calles is from Valencia County, the daughter of Adolfo and Lola Calles of Rio Communities. She is an artist who also works for the Catholic church in Las Vegas while de Aragon himself is employed as a bilingual specialist for the Los Lunas schools and teaches Spanish at the Valencia Campus. She will be on a panel addressing "The State of the Indo-Hispano Arts in Nuevo Mexico."

He's a santero and fine artist, using oil and acrylic in his paintings, which usually have a religious theme.

The association's luncheon is by invitation only, and he'll speak mostly to an audience of artists and others involved in the art world. Among the other speakers will be novelist Rudolfo Anaya, Soledad Campos of the Smithsonian Institution, and Penny Ojeda of the National Endowment for the Arts.

Ray John de Aragon
Speaking at conference

"I won't be touching just folk art but the fine arts. And I'll be talking about the problems Hispanic artists found in being recognized and shown in galleries."

Ray John de Aragon
Author and artist

The National Association for Latino Arts and Culture sponsors conferences that draw attention to nationally recognized artists and authors. The one in Albuquerque recognized the works of Rudolfo Anaya and Ray John de Aragón. *Author's collection.*

Above: Corky Gonzales and his wife, Geraldine, in Las Vegas, New Mexico, in 1971. They joined a student march protesting employment practices at the university. Corky's epic poem "I Am Joaquin" served as a battle cry for the national Chicano movement. *Photo by Adelita Medina.*

Left: Noted New Mexico photographer Arnold Trujillo captured land grant leader Tijerina in this image at New Mexico Highlands University's Ilfeld Auditorium. "I was so excited to show this social justice hero in quiet reflection by conveying on film a respect and admiration that I felt." *Courtesy Arnold Trujillo.*

were seen on posters and banners flyers along with others that proclaimed, "The March of the Poor for Justice, Work, Bread, and Liberty, Long Live the Union of the Poor!" The struggle for justice in the Chicano movement was developed and spurred on by Reies López Tijerina. His passionate outcry was picked up by other civil rights leaders of the period, such as Corky Gonzales of Denver, Colorado, and José Ángel Gutiérrez. Rodolfo "Corky" Gonzales formed his Crusade for Justice in Colorado in 1966. Many joined in both in New Mexico and across America.

Nelson Mandela's vibrant words continue to resonate when he said:

> *Real leaders must be ready to sacrifice all for the freedom of the people.... The dire poverty of some is not an affliction which impacts only on those who are deprived. It reverberates across the globe and ineluctably impacts negatively on the whole of humanity, including those who live in conditions of comfort and plenty....I have cherished the ideal of a democratic and free society in which all persons live together in harmony and with equal opportunities....As long as poverty, injustice, and gross inequality persists in our world, none of us can truly rest.*

Mandela fought against a system of racial segregation and discrimination in South Africa. He died fighting.

In New Mexico and the rest of the country, civil rights and justice leaders did not rest. They did not take the easy way out with inactivity, relaxation or sleep. They were not motionless or silent. They did not lie down. They sought to improve social conditions and fought against institutional policies that were detrimental to the public, policies that ignored and desecrated core principles and values. These leaders encouraged grassroots empowerment.

They used positive strategies and tactics such as rallies, marches, sit-ins and peaceful assembly to generate awareness of social issues for marginalized groups. They promoted a paradigm shift in thoughts and actions aimed at the common good. They encouraged risks and nonviolence. At times, they were lonely voices on the fringe of society. They continued to speak out until they caught the public attention with their words and actions. They organized, educated and involved everyone in a common goal. The objectives were to correct past injustices, improve the present and hopefully create an environment of equality for everyone.

BIBLIOGRAPHY

Acuña, Rodolfo. *Occupied America: The Chicano's Struggle Toward Liberation*. San Francisco: Canfield Press, 1972.

Bernard, Jacqueline. *Voices from the Southwest: Antonio José Martínez, Elfego Baca, Reies López Tijerina*. New York: Firebird Books, Scholastic Book Service, 1972.

Blawis, Patricia Bell. *Tijerina and the Land Grants: Mexican American Struggle for Their Heritage*. New York: International Publishers, 1987.

Busto, Rudy V. *King Tiger: The Religious Vision of Reies López Tijerina*. Albuquerque: University of New Mexico Press, 2005.

Cather, Willa. *Death Comes for the Archbishop*. New York: Vintage Books, 1990.

Chávez, Fray Angélico. *But Time and Chance: The Story of Padre Martínez of Taos, 1793–1867*. Santa Fe, NM: Sunstone Press, 1981.

De Aragón, Ray John. *Padre Martínez and Bishop Lamy*. Las Vegas, NM: Pan American Publishing Company, 1976.

Dunbar-Ortiz. *Roots of Resistance: A History of Land Tenure in New Mexico*. Norman: University of Oklahoma Press, 2007.

Gardner, Richard. *¡Grito! Reies López Tijerina and the New Mexico Land Grant War of 1967*. Indianapolis, IN: Bobbs-Merrill Company, 1970.

Gonzales, Berry, and David R. Maciel. *The Contested Homeland: A Chicano History of New Mexico*. Albuquerque: University of New Mexico Press, 2000.

Griswold del Castillo, Richard. *The Treaty of Guadalupe Hidalgo: A Legacy of Conflict*. Norman: University of Oklahoma Press, 1990.

Hall, Edward T. *The Hidden Dimension*. New York: Doubleday and Co., 1969.

Hofstadter, Richard. *Social Darwinism in American Thought*. Boston: Beacon Press, 1959.

Horgan, Paul. *Lamy of Santa Fe: His Life and Times*. New York: Farrar, Straus and Giroux, 1975.

Marder, William. *Indians in the Americas: The Untold Story*. San Diego, CA: Book Tree, 2005.

Mares, E.A. *I Returned and Saw Under the Sun: Padre Martínez of Taos*. Albuquerque: University of New Mexico Press, 1989.

Martínez, Elizabeth, ed. *500 Years of Chicano History in Pictures*. Albuquerque: New Mexico Southwest Organizing Project, 1991.

McWilliams, Carey. *North from Mexico: The Spanish Speaking People in the United States*. New York: Greenwood Press, 1968.

Miller, Darlis. "Foragers, Army Women, and Prostitutes." In *New Mexico Women: An Intercultural Perspective*, edited by Darlis Miller and Joan M. Jensen. Albuquerque: University of New Mexico Press, 1986, 124.

Nabokov, Peter. *Tijerina and the Courthouse Raid*. Albuquerque: University of New Mexico Press, 1969.

Powell, Philip Wayne. *Tree of Hate: Propaganda and Prejudices Affecting United States Relations with the Hispanic World*. New York: Basic Books, 1971.

Rosenbaum, J. Robert. *Mexicano Resistance in the Southwest*. Austin: University of Texas Press, 1986.

Salaz, Ruben Dario. *Cosmic: The La Raza Sketchbook*. Santa Fe, NM: Blue Feather Press, 1975.

Simmons, M. *New Mexico: An Interpretive History*. Albuquerque: University of New Mexico Press, 1988.

Spicer, Edward H. *Cycles of Conquest*. Tucson: University of Arizona Press, 1962.

Tijerina, Reies López. *Mi Lucha Por La Tierra*. Mexico, Distrito Federal: Fondo de Cultura Económica, 1978.

———. *The Spanish Land Grant Problem Examined*. Albuquerque, NM: Alianza Federal de Mercedes, 1966.

Tijerina, Reies López, translated and edited by José Ángel Gutiérrez. *They Called Me "King Tiger": My Struggle for the Land and Our Rights*. Houston, TX: Arte Publico Press, 2000.

Ulibarri, Sabine R. *Tierra Amarilla: Stories of New Mexico*. Albuquerque: University of New Mexico Press, 1993.

ABOUT THE AUTHOR

As a high school student, Ray John de Aragón got caught up in the drama, sorrow, racism and despair of the 1960s. While glued to the ongoing print and television media of the day, he lived through and relived the assassination of President Kennedy, the struggles in Alabama and the voice of Dr. Martin Luther King Jr. and others espousing civil rights and justice. This left a profound impact on his coming-of-age experiences. After graduation, he joined the Alianza Federal de las Mercedes, led by land grant leader Reies López Tijerina, in May 1967, just before the Tierra Amarilla Courthouse Raid. After a stint in Vietnam, Ray John became a student activist at the University of Albuquerque. He worked under a program sponsored by Lyndon Baines Johnson's Great Society as a student and then became the Student Senate's activities vice president in charge of managing all entertainment, recreation and speaker events for students on campus. As a student/employee, de Aragón was directly under the office of university president Dr. Frank Kleinhenz with a working budget. He hired performing groups such as the well-known bands El Chicano, Zozobra and others. Speakers he selected included

Tijerina, Dr. Sabine Ulibarri, New Mexico news media icon José Armas, radio and music personality and Lieutenant Governor Roberto Mondragón and representatives of the Black Berets and other civil rights organizations. Some events were cosponsored with La Raza Educators Association, a large Hispanic teacher and education administrator organization in Albuquerque. Ray John became president of the Associated Students of U of A. He then fought for the hiring of a Hispanic president at New Mexico Highlands University in his hometown of Las Vegas. Ray John de Aragón holds an advanced degree in American Studies. He has lectured at various universities and colleges and has been a keynote speaker at conferences speaking on issues adversely affecting Hispanic populations in New Mexico and the country.